Apples of Gold

A Devotional in Rhyme

Denise Jeter

Copyright © 2009 by Denise Jeter

Apples of Gold
by Denise Jeter

Printed in the United States of America

ISBN 9781615793914

All rights reserved solely by the author. The author guarantees all contents are original and do not infringe upon the legal rights of any other person or work. No part of this book may be reproduced in any form without the permission of the author. The views expressed in this book are not necessarily those of the publisher.

Unless otherwise indicated, Bible quotations are taken from King James Version of the Bible. Copyright © 1997 by World Publishing Inc.

www.xulonpress.com

Dedication

*To my wonderful husband, Shane who has
supported me and been there for me through
thick and thin*

*To my precious son, Cody who is truly
the light of my life*

Acknowledgments

I want to first thank my Lord and Savior Jesus Christ for all things

Also I want to thank my very special friend Felicia M. Lyons, without whom this book would not exist

Testimonial

I would like to tell you how much your "Apples of Gold" devotional really became a blessing to me and Ann. Let me explain. About three weeks ago Dean Hodgson who is my wife's brother came up missing from the care center he had been staying at. Dean has had two live in care givers for most of his adult life because of his mental illness that developed in his early twenties; he is now sixty-two years old. And when he disappeared from the care center in Houston they contacted us and we immediately began to try to find him. To say it was like looking for a needle in a haystack is a big understatement. We created color photo flyers and posted them in all the areas he was known to frequently visit even though he was living at the care center he had the freedom to leave during the day to go to the store, fast food places, etc. He had lived at care centers for many years and had never disappeared like this. .We searched all over and even contacted the news media (TV stations) with no success. The police also had a missing person report on him and they were looking

Apples of Gold

for him too. By the third day Ann was getting frantic and we were about at our wits end, even though both of us kept saying we trusted in God to help us find him. Then on Friday morning Ann received one of your "Apples of Gold" messages and it was from the scripture reference "1 Samuel 11:9 - Tomorrow, by the time the sun be hot, ye shall have help." Well Ann just clung to that promise and we just kept searching even late that night. Saturday the next day we were so tired, but we were still searching and clinging to God's promise. Late Saturday evening (and the sun was sure hot here in Houston in July) Ann received a call from Texas Equa Search and they agreed to help us search. They were such a blessing. They came out Sunday the next day with what looked like a small army and helped us search diligently for Dean. Without going into all the details, Dean was found on that very day and we couldn't thank Our Lord Jesus enough for His help and the help He sent our way and for the promise He gave to us through your ministry. Ironically the scripture you shared in the "Apples of Gold" the day we found Dean was " 1 Samuel 12:16 - Now therefore stand see this great thing, which the Lord will do before your eyes." May the Lord continue using you in His service and I know many others will be blessed by your ministry.

Pastor William Wesson,
Calvary Tabernacle
Deer Park, Texas

Preface

I am not a theologian by any stretch of the imagination, nor do I profess to be. The truths that are to be found on the following pages were born out of blood, sweat and tears at times and were taught me by the Holy Spirit. God in his infinite wisdom allowed me to walk through places in life where if I was going to survive them, I was going to have to learn the Lord's ways and truths to make it through.

My hope is that as you walk through these pages day by day they will help you know the truth that the truth might set you free, and give you a new understanding of the words, "The letter killeth, but the Spirit maketh alive."

May the Lord bless you and Keep you and make His face to shine upon you.

Apples of Gold

January 1

1 Corinthians 6:20

"For ye are bought with a price: therefore glorify God in your body, and in your spirit, which are God's."

You were bought with a price
More precious than gold
The righteous blood of Jesus
Was the price of your soul

So glorify the Lord
In all you say and do
Because of the great sacrifice
He has made for me and you

Apples of Gold

January 2

Galatians 6:7-8

"Be not deceived; God is not mocked: for whatsoever a man soweth, that shall he also reap. For he that soweth to his flesh shall of the flesh reap corruption; but he that soweth to the Spirit shall of the Spirit reap life everlasting."

You can't sow one thing
And reap another
So be careful, very careful
How you treat your brother

All that we sow
We shall also reap
So may we be watchful
The commandments to keep

But when we stumble
From this great task
For his grace and mercy
We simply must ask

Apples of Gold

January 3

Hebrews 5:8

"Though he were a Son, yet learned he obedience by the things which he suffered;"

If Jesus Christ, through suffering learned
How he should obey
Should we not embrace our cross
That will cause us not to stray

David said it was good for me
That I have been afflicted
Because in the end, this little trial
Will keep me from being rejected

Apples of Gold

January 4

1 John 3:17

"But whoso hath this world's good, and seeth his brother have need, and shutteth up his bowels of compassion from him, how dewelleth the love of God in him?"

When we see our brother
Who's in desperate need
Let us not hesitate
Our brother to clothe and feed

That is what the Lord
Has instructed us to do
The day he washed and clothed us
And made us all brand new

Apples of Gold

January 5

Revelation 13:16-17

"And he causeth all, both small and great, rich and poor, free and bond, to receive a mark in their right hand, or in their foreheads: And that no man might buy or sell, save he that had the mark, or the name of the beast, or the number of his name."

The Antichrist, he has a plan
Of that you can be sure
He wants us all to receive a mark
It's a simple, subtle lure

But those who receive the mark
Their torment, will end no never
Revelation fourteen eleven
Tells of this endeavor

Apples of Gold

January 6

Revelation 20:15

"And whosoever was not found written in the book of life was cast into the lake of fire."

There's coming a day, a dreaded day
When all things will be shown
The ones whose names are written down
Will be ever before his throne

But there will be another group
Who have never called on Jesus
And that group, eternally damned
That day they will have to leave us

Apples of Gold

January 7

Jeremiah 5:25

"Your iniquities have turned away these things, and your sins have withholden good things from you."

Sometimes we forget
The things we say and do
Can prevent the blessing
From coming straight to you

The Father has them ready
To deliver them with cheer
But our lack of our repentance
Keeps them from us I fear

Apples of Gold

January 8

Mark 1:17

"...There cometh one mightier than I after me, the latchet of whose shoes I am not worthy to stoop down and unloose."

Come after me
I have a job for you
To be fishers of men
Is what I would have you to do

There are some fish In your pond
That others cannot reach
If you will hearken to my words
How to catch them, I will teach

Apples of Gold

January 9

Galatians 6:2

"Bear ye one another's burdens, and so fulfil the law of Christ."

If there is a burden
You can help your brother bear
Be quick to offer your help
And show him that you care

When other's look away
You can show Christ love
And glorify our Father
Who's watching from heaven above

Apples of Gold

January 10

1 Timothy 2:12

"But I suffer not a woman to teach, nor to usurp authority over the man, but to be in silence."

God has a perfect order
We tend to forget
And Satan uses this
To trap us in his net

He used it in the garden
When he tempted Eve
And shortly thereafter
From the garden, they had to leave

Apples of Gold

January 11

Philemon vs. 15

"For perhaps he therefore departed for a season, that thou shouldest receive him for ever."

Sometimes our children wander
Sometimes our children stray
Sometimes the Lord is working
So in the kingdom they will stay

At times the Lord must show them
The world is a scary place
So that when they return to him
They will seek only his face

Apples of Gold

January 12

James 1:23-24

"For if any be a hearer of the word, and not a doer, he is like unto a man beholding his natural face in a glass; For he beholdeth himself, and goeth his way, and straightway forgetteth what manner of man he was."

There is a danger to be found
In only hearing the word
If we do not practice what we hear
These principles will not work

So be ye not a hearer only
But these words put into practice
Or we shall find, that very truly
Satan will attack us

Apples of Gold

January 13

1 Chronicles 17:2

"...Do all that is in thine heart; for God is with thee."

Go forward with the thoughts
That dwell within your heart
For I shall be with you
At the finish as well as the start

As I was with Moses
So shall I be with thee
To watch and protect you
From the enemy

Apples of Gold

January 14

Psalms 50:16

"But unto the wicked God saith, What hast thou to do to declare my statutes, or that thou shouldest take my covenant in thy mouth?"

Bible quoting sinners
They everywhere abound
The Lord hears every word
And truly detest that sound

They bring reproach
To his Holy name
And shall one day
Of their deeds be ashamed

Apples of Gold

January 15

Exodus 18:11

"Now I know that the Lord is greater than all gods; for in the thing wherein they dealt proudly he was above them.:

The proud may rant and rave
Try to bring you down
But God's still on the throne
And God still wears the crown

The wicked they may try
To carry out their master plan
Over time we'll see the judgment
Of all plans of man

Apples of Gold

January 16

Ezekiel 21:16

"Go thee one way or other, either on the right hand, or the left, whithersoever thy face is set."

Joshua said to choose
This day whom you will serve
I pray you will choose Jesus
Our praise and worship he deserves

We must make a choice
To go left or right
Just keep in mind the path we choose
Is well within his sight

Apples of Gold

January 17

Acts 13:2

"As they ministered to the Lord, and fasted, the Holy Ghost said, Separate me Barnabas and Saul for the work whereunto I have called them."

Unsure of your calling
Unsure what to do
If you seek the Lord with fasting
It will become clearer to you

Fasting is a weapon
Not very often tried
It has enough power
To make Satan run and hide

Apples of Gold

January 18

Hebrews 4:15-16

"For we have not an high priest which cannot be touched with the feeling of our infirmities; but was in all points tempted like as we are yet without sin. Let us therefore come boldly unto the throne of grace, that we may obtain mercy, and find grace to help in time of need."

Jesus is our high priest
He knows how we feel
He knows all our short comings
And with what we have to deal

That's why He rent the veil
And made for us a way
To come to the father
And ask for help today

Apples of Gold

January 19

1 Peter 4:8

"And above all things have fervent charity among yourselves; for charity shall cover the multitude of sins."

When our brother stumbles
And is about to fall
Don't forget to love them
It could be us after all

We have all fallen short
Of the glory of God
May we be kind to one another
While upon the earth we trod

Apples of Gold

January 20

Genesis 32:24

"And Jacob was left alone; and there wrestled a man with him until the breaking of the day."

Our mind may wrestle
With the words from above
In time God will instruct us
By his great mercy and love

If there is a passage
We cannot understand
Let us hold fast to God
Who will always hold our hand

Apples of Gold

January 21

Lamentations 3:25

"The Lord is good unto them that wait for him, to the soul that seeketh him."

At times we must wait
Maybe a year or two
Before we see the promises
Coming into view

They that wait upon the Lord
Shall never loose their strength
Let us never give up on God
No matter what we think

Apples of Gold

January 22

2 Chronicles 20:6

"...O Lord God of our fathers, art not thou God in heaven? And rulest not thou over all the kingdoms of the heathen? And in thine hand is there not power and might, so that none is able to withstand thee?"

God holds all power
In the palm of his hand
Having had all power
Since time began

There is no power in heaven
Or here on earth
That can thwart his love for you
Or diminish your worth

Apples of Gold

January 23

Jeremiah 10:2

"Thus saith the Lord, learn not the way of the heathen, and be not dismayed at the signs of heaven; for the heathen are dismayed at them."

We shall see signs from heaven
As the end draws near
And though these signs be mighty
Do not give in to fear

They simply mean the Lord
Is truly on his way
And that upon this earth
Not much longer shall we stay

Apples of Gold

January 24

Daniel 11:32

"…the people that do know their God shall be strong, and do exploits."

As the end draws closer
With every passing day
The saints of God grow stronger
In every single way

We shall do great exploits
As we follow him
We must keep our focus
And not follow every whim

Apples of Gold

January 25

Luke 1:45

"And blessed is she that believed;
for there shall be a performance of those
things which were told her from
the Lord."

If we believe the scriptures
We shall be blessed indeed
And our prayers shall be answered
When we are in need

Ours is but to believe
And obey
From our Fathers gaze
We are not to stray

Apples of Gold

January 26

John 7:7

"The world cannot hate you; but me it hateth, because I testify of it, that the works thereof are evil."

Men love darkness
Rather than light
Prefer to do wrong
Rather than right

That's why men hate Jesus
And want that precious name banned
They try to take it from our schools
And drive it from our land

Apples of Gold

January 27

Romans 3:23

"For all have sinned, and come short of the glory of God;"

There's not one good
No not one
So we've been told
So saith the Son

All have fallen short
Of the glory of God
But his grace is sufficient
While on this earth we trod

Apples of Gold

January 28

Galatians 1:9

"As we said before, so say I now again, If any man preach any other gospel unto you than that ye have received, let him be accursed."

There are many false prophets
Other gospels they preach
They have no sound doctrine
And it's lies that they teach

So when in doubt
Run to the Bible
In these last days
It's our hope of survival

Apples of Gold

January 29

Mark 2:17

"...They that are whole have no need of
the physician, but they that are sick;
I came not to call the righteous,
but sinners to repentance,"

Jesus came not to condemn
But he came to save the lost
So that you might be with him in heaven
No matter what the cost

So turn your eyes toward Jesus
The one who is able to save
He that bought you with blood
And then came out of the grave

Apples of Gold

January 30

Acts 13:2

"As they ministered to the Lord, and fasted, the Holy Ghost said, Separate me Barnabas and Saul for the work whereunto I have called them."

For those who need direction
Who seek the right path for their feet
If you will but fast and pray
The Father's plan you will meet

There may be turns and twists
Along the narrow way
But following the plan of God
Will lead to a brighter day

Apples of Gold

January 31

Hebrews 12:28

"Wherefore we receiving a kingdom which cannot be moved, let us have grace, whereby we may serve God acceptably with reverence and godly fear;"

We must serve the Lord with reverence
We must serve the Lord with fear
Fall not into the current trend
But hold the old paths near

There is a group who are falling away
They've gone the way of entertainment
They put on shows and plays
But hold not to the commandments

Apples of Gold

February 1

1 John 4:4

Ye are of God , little children, and have overcome them; because greater is he that is in you, than he that is in the world."

Satan likes to make you think
That he has more power than you
But I came by to tell you
That just isn't true

If we are born again
Living our life in Jesus
We have all power in heaven and earth
And it's that power that frees us

Apples of Gold

February 2

1 John 3:17

"But whoso hath this world's good, and seeth his brother have need, and shutteth up his bowels of compassion from him, how dwelleth the love of God in him?"

If you have the means to help your brother
But look the other way
The love of God dwells not in you
And you have gone astray

But if you seek your brothers best
And try to meet his need
The Father will open the windows
of blessing
And pour them on you indeed

Apples of Gold

February 3

1 John 4:1

"Beloved, believe not every spirit, but try the spirits whether they are of God; because many false prophets are gone out into the world."

Test what you hear
Test what you see
So that by a false spirit
Deceived you will not be

Many who profess
The God of heaven
Have mixed in their doctrine
A little leaven

Apples of Gold

February 4

1 John 4:18

"There is no fear in love; but perfect love casteth out fear; because fear hath torment. He that feareth is not made perfect in love"

If the enemy
Is bringing on you fear
Through your thoughts
Or through those you hold dear

This my friend
Is not the work of God
We must take our authority
And over the enemy trod

Apples of Gold

February 5

2 Kings 8:6

"...Restore all that was hers, and all the fruits of the field since the day that she left the land, even until now."

Have you left the things of God
To see what the world had to offer
If you will but return to him
He'll shut the mouth of the scoffers

For he is the God that will restore
And give back all you've lost
Because, for all our backslidings
He paid the awful cost

Apples of Gold

February 6

Psalms 139:17-18

"How precious also are thy thoughts unto me, O God! How great is the sum of them! If I should count them they are more in number than the sand; when I awake, I am still with thee."

The thoughts of the Lord toward us
Are more than the sands of the sea
What have we done to deserve this
Why does he love you and me

He loves us because he made us
And he is watching over us now
And if we long to please him
He will surely show us how

Apples of Gold

February 7

John 20:25

"...Except I shall see in his hands the print of the nails, and put my finger into the print of the nails, and thrust my hand into his side, I will not believe."

Don't be unbelieving
Like our brother Thomas
But run to the open arms of God
And receive his wonderful promise

He has promised to save and restore you
In his holy word he said
You shall live forever
As I am now living, though I were dead

Apples of Gold

February 8

1 Corinthians 15:58

"Therefore, my beloved brethren, be ye steadfast, unmoveable, always abounding in the work of the Lord, forasmuch as ye know that your labor is not in vain in the Lord."

No matter what you see
No matter what you feel
If your labor is for the Lord
Your reward will be very real

You may not see the profit
You may not see the gain
But your Father is watching
And he sees all your pain

Apples of Gold

February 9

Acts 22:15

"For thou shalt be his witness unto all men of what thou hast seen and heard."

What have you watched
Your master do
These miracles you've seen
Were not just for you

We must share with others
And speak of his great power
For the rapture is approaching
Yes, that very hour

Apples of Gold

February 10

Ephesians 2:10

"For we are his workmanship, created in Christ Jesus unto good works, which God hath before ordained that we should walk in them."

The works He has for you
Have already been laid out
Ours is but to seek his face
And his praises tout

We should try to remember
This little verse in Ephesians
So when the enemy taunts us
We can say our life has a reason

Apples of Gold

February 11

Ephesians 4:7

But unto every one of us is given grace according to the measure of the gift of Christ."

We all have a different calling
So we all have different grace
You will understand your measure
When you see him face to face

And face to face, you will see him
On that judgment day
To receive your reward from his hand
Or to be bid, from me go away

Apples of Gold

February 12

Luke 22:31-32

"And the Lord said, Simon, Simon, behold, Satan hath desired to have you, that he may sift you as wheat: But I have prayed for thee, that thy faith fail not: and when thou art converted, strengthen thy brethren."

Satan is not happy
When we leave his fold
And will do all in his power
To hold on to your soul

But Jesus will pray for you
Just as he did for Simon
For you are more precious to him
Than the most costly diamond

Apples of Gold

February 13

Romans 8:31

"What shall we say then to these things?
If God be for us, who can be against us?"

If God be for you
Then who can thwart his plan
Not devils or principalities
Not even wicked man

For if the Lord
Is on your side
To the very gates of heaven
He will be your guide

Apples of Gold

February 14

Ephesians 4:26-27

"Be ye angry, and sin not: let not the sun go down upon your wrath; Neither give place to the devil."

The enemy desires a place
In your house and in your soul
But keeping him away
Must be one of our goals

For if we let the sun
Go down on our wrath
We should not be surprised
To find the devil in our path

Apples of Gold

February 15

Colossians 2:8

"Beware lest any man spoil you through philosophy and vain deceit, after the tradition of men, after the rudiments of the world, and not after Christ."

There are some teachers
With words so lofty
They call it the gospel
But really it's philosophy

It sounds really good
To the human ear
But when sifted through the scriptures
Only chaff will appear

Apples of Gold

February 16

Titus 1:16

"They profess that they know God; but in works they deny him, being abominable, and disobedient, and unto every good work reprobate."

Professors are a dime a dozen
You can find them everywhere
But when it comes to obeying God
They absolutely, have no fear

They talk it up good
Put on a good show
Taking no thought of the day
When the proud will be brought low

Apples of Gold

February 17

Hebrews 11:15

"And truly, if they had been mindful of that country from whence they came out, they might have had opportunity to have returned."

If you've been delivered
From this world of woe
Don't think of returning
Remember your foe

Once you've put your hand to the plow
There is no looking back
For all that lies behind us
Is vanity and lack

Apples of Gold

February 18

Jude vs. 3

"Beloved, when I gave all diligence to write unto you of the common salvation, it was needful for me to write unto you, and exhort you that ye should earnestly contend for the faith which was once delivered unto the saints."

There are some subverting
Trying to twist the word
Trying to make it say something
You've never even heard

We must stand against them
Contend at all cost
Because nothing on this planet
Is worth what could be lost

Apples of Gold

February 19

Psalms 41:1-2

"Blessed is he that considereth the poor: the Lord will deliver him in time of trouble. The Lord will preserve him, and keep him alive; and he shall be blessed upon the earth: and thou wilt not deliver him unto the will of his enemies."

If to the poor you are mindful
You can rest assured
That God is watching over you
And blessings, they are yours

And though your foes be many
And trials not a few
The Lord will deliver
And surely rescue you

Apples of Gold

February 20

Deuteronomy 4:37

"And because he loved thy fathers, therefore he chose their seed after them, and brought thee out in his sight with his mighty power out of Egypt;"

Because of those who came before
These blessings do we reap
Because our fathers served the Lord
Their children will he keep

To many generations
Do these blessings flow
From our fathers and our grandfathers
To our children do they go

Apples of Gold

February 21

Genesis 41:51

"…For God, said he, hath made me forget all my toil, and all my father's house."

When God begins to bless us
We forget all of our trials
Because the blessings over take us
And redeem those weary miles

All those years we waited
For the promise to come true
Now seem like mere moments
For he is blessing all we do

Apples of Gold

February 22

Genesis 41:52

"...For God hath caused me to be fruitful in the land of my affliction."

My affliction is what God used
To teach me his precious ways
And for the massive struggle
I will be thankful all my days

His ways are not our ways
They seem upside down
And we won't understand them
Until we receive our crown

Apples of Gold

February 23

Exodus 1:21

**"And it came to pass,
because the midwives feared God,
that he made them houses."**

The midwives feared the Lord
More than they feared the king
And ultimately this decision
Would cause their hearts to sing

God always provides
For those who fear his word
And of his provision
They can rest assured

Apples of Gold

February 24

Exodus 3:7

"And the Lord said,
I have surely seen the affliction of my people which are in Egypt, and have heard their cry by reason of their taskmasters; for I know their sorrows;"

Your sorrows have been seen and heard
By the one who sees it all
And he is very near
To those, who on him call

So if your taskmasters
Are showing you their power
Believe that your Father
With blessings, will soon shower

Apples of Gold

February 25

Numbers 13:30

"And Caleb stilled the people before Moses, and said, Let us go up at once, and possess it; for we are well able to overcome it."

When the Lord is with us
We can take possession
Overcome the greatest foe
And teach those watching a lesson

It is better to believe God
Than to have the smallest doubt
Had they doubted in Jericho
They would have had no reason to shout

Apples of Gold

February 26

Revelation 2: 2 and 4

"I know thy works and thy labor, and thy patience, and how thou canst not bear them which are evil;"…Nevertheless I have somewhat against thee, because thou hast left thy first love."

Don't let the rules and laws
Make you forget the man
Who delivered you from evil
And took you by the hand

His hand is still stretched outward
He still wants to forgive
And desires that in his presence
You would daily live

Apples of Gold

February 27

3 John vs. 11

"Beloved, follow not that which is evil, but that which is good. He that doeth good is of God; but he that doeth evil hath not seen God."

We're not to follow a multitude
Into their evil deeds
We must follow the Lord
For he will meet our needs

For those who follow Jesus
Must try to be like him
And not be blinded by this world
Nor allow our eyes to dim

Apples of Gold

February 28

1 John 4:12

"No man hath seen God at any time..."

Many are saying in this day
They have seen the face of God
But according to this scripture
On shaky ground they trod

So if their little stories
Don't match the Bible here
Makes you wonder if they reverence
And hold the scriptures dear

Apples of Gold

March 1

1 John 2:16-17

"For all that is in the world, the lust of the flesh, and the lust of the eyes, and the pride of life, is not of the Father, but is of the world. And the world passeth away, and the lust thereof; but he that doeth the will of God abideth for ever."

The bright lights of the world
They tend to entice
But given free rein
They will but, lead to vice

But if we follow Jesus
His reward is so much better
For we will be in heaven
With him, forever and ever

Apples of Gold

March 2

2 Peter 2:19

"...For of whom a man is overcome, of the same is he brought in bondage."

When we submit our members
To a dastardly deed
In order to overcome
Miraculous help we will need

For once, Satan snares you
You cannot free yourself
Supernatural Intervention
Can provide the only help

Apples of Gold

March 3

2 Peter 2:9

"The Lord knoweth how to deliver the godly out of temptations…"

If you've fallen in a trap
Of which you cannot break free
Run to the Lord with all your might
Make known your urgent plea

He will in no wise
Cast you away
But surely deliver you
This very day

Apples of Gold

March 4

1 Peter 5:5

"Likewise, ye younger, submit yourselves unto the elder. Yea, all of you be subject one to another; and be clothed with humility; for God resisteth the proud, and giveth grace to the humble."

Submit, Submit, Submit
The sweetest word I know
By giving up we win the war
And gain victory over our foe

It sounds a little upside down
And backward, that's a fact
But if you take this keen advice
You'll thwart off this attack

Apples of Gold

March 5

Matthew 4:4

"...It is written, Man shall not live by bread alone, but by every word that proceedeth out of the mouth of God."

Bread alone, all by itself
Will never see us through
The darkness of this lonely world
Closing in on you

We must have bread from heaven
And that bread is Jesus
For when we hunger after him
He surely feeds us

Apples of Gold

March 6

Matthew 4:16

"The people which sat in darkness saw great light; and to them which sat in the region and shadow of death light is sprung up."

When we think all hope is gone
We could not be more mistaken
For when we're at our lowest point
We are not forsaken

The darker things become
Closer comes the light
And if we will but lift our eyes
Jesus will be in sight

Apples of Gold

March 7

Matthew 4:17

"From that time Jesus began to preach, and to say, Repent: for the kingdom of heaven is at hand."

Jesus is closer
Than he has ever been before
If you have a listening ear
You will hear him at the door

He's saying time is getting shorter
The end is drawing nigh
Repent while there's still time
I'm soon coming back from on high

Apples of Gold

March 8

Matthew 5:16

"Let your light so shine before men, that they may see your good works, and glorify your Father which is in heaven."

Don't hide what's inside you
Let it shine before men
They must see your Father
Before time comes to an end

So use your days wisely
To win all you can
Because soon we will give an account
And before his throne, we will stand

Apples of Gold

March 9

Matthew 6:16

"Moreover when ye fast, be not, as the hypocrites, of a sad countenance; for they disfigure their faces, that they may appear unto men to fast, Verily I say unto you, They have their reward,"

Fast not to be seen of men
But to be seen of your Father
Who from heaven will reward you
And promote you like no other

Men can give a small reward
But God's reward is forever
Eternity is a long time
Lasting forever and ever

Apples of Gold

March 10

Matthew 6:24

"No man can serve two masters; for either he will hate the one, and love the other; or else he will hold to the one, and despise the other. Ye cannot serve God and mammon."

We cannot serve God
And also serve our dollars
No matter what false teachers say
Or all those professing scholars

Many have gone the way of Balaam
And sold out for treasure
It will not be worth the cost
When eternity they begin to measure

Apples of Gold

March 11

Matthew 6:31

"Therefore take no thought, saying what shall we eat? Or, What shall we drink? Or, Wherewithal shall we be clothed?"

Worry not for your daily needs
Because your Father sees
Exactly what you have need of
And intends to meet your needs

He will provide your food
And he will provide your drink
So seek ye first the kingdom
And on him often think

Apples of Gold

March 12

Psalms 5:12

"For thou, Lord, wilt bless the righteous;
with favor wilt thou compass him
as with a shield."

When people give you favor
And like you quite well
Give you special privileges
More than you can tell

You need to look beyond yourself
And know it is not you
It is God almighty
Who is blessing all you do

Apples of Gold

March 13

Proverbs 14:12

"There is a way which seemeth right unto a man, but the end thereof are the ways of death."

Many things look logical
Many things sound right
But if you really want the truth
You must ask God for insight

For many things glitter
That are not true gold
In order to find our way
We must follow the paths of old

Apples of Gold

March 14

Isaiah 19:20

"...They shall cry unto the Lord because of the oppressors, and he shall send them a saviour, and a great one, and he shall deliver them."

Is something oppressing you
A person, place or thing
Take it to the Lord
He's ruler over everything

His name is above sickness
His name is above drink
His name is above drugs
Or anything you can think

Apples of Gold

March 15

Jeremiah 10:12

"He hath made the earth by his power, he hath established the world by his wisdom, and hath stretched out the heavens by his discretion."

If you think the Lord
Cannot solve your problem
Read this little verse
Then tell him why he can't solve them

If we just take a moment to consider
What the Lord has already done
We'll see that no blessing will he withhold
Since he did not withhold his Son

Apples of Gold

March 16

Jeremiah 51:36

"Therefore thus saith the Lord; Behold, I will plead thy cause, and take vengeance for thee; ..."

We need not avenge ourselves
For we have an avenger
His name is Jesus Christ
This we should remember

Vengeance is mine, thus saith the Lord
He will repay in due season
And when the wicked wonder why
He will remind them of the reason

Apples of Gold

March 17

Daniel 2:28

"But there is a God in heaven that revealeth secrets…"

Things that are impossible, to us
To think or ever know
He knows all about them
And has them in control

He sets up kings and bring them down
And when it's all said and done
We'll understand and see the wisdom
Of the movement of every one

Apples of Gold

March 18

2 Samuel 15:11

"And with Absalom went two hundred men out of Jerusalem, that were called; and they went in their simplicity, and they knew not any thing."

To follow someone blindly
Is to make a sad mistake
If we don't check out the messenger
Our end may be to hard to take

Let us be like the bereans
Who searched the scripture every day
And check out the messengers
And every word they say

Apples of Gold

March 19

Jeremiah 32:27

"Behold, I am the Lord the God of all flesh; is there any thing too hard for me?"

What is too hard for God
What is there that he cannot do
It's not above his ability
Even when it's too hard for you

He hung the world on nothing
He flung the stars in space
He gave to us the seasons
And put everything in place

Apples of Gold

March 20

Daniel 2:21

"And he changeth the times and the seasons; he removeth kings, and setteth up kings; he giveth wisdom unto the wise, and knowledge to them that know understanding;"

He sets them up
He brings them down
When all seems lost
He declares it found

He passes out knowledge
And gives wisdom to the wise
And nothing is hidden
From his all seeing eyes

Apples of Gold

March 21

Jonah 2:7

"When my soul fainted within me
I remembered the Lord: and my prayer
came in unto thee, into thine
holy temple."

When our soul has fainted
And all seems to be lost
Remember how he bought us back
Remember what it cost

If he has brought us this far
He will not leave us behind
For when we stray from the fold
He leaves the ninety-nine

Apples of Gold

March 22

Habakkuk 3:17-18

"Although the fig tree shall not blossom, neither shall fruit be in the vines; the labour of the olive shall fail, and the fields shall yield no meat; the flock shall be cut off from the fold, and there shall be no herd in the stalls: Yet I will rejoice in the Lord, I will joy in the God of my salvation."

When things look really bleak
And all hope seems gone
Remember it's always darkest
Right before the dawn

Rejoice in the Lord
Again I say rejoice
For at your lowest moment
You'll here your Fathers voice

Apples of Gold

March 23

Haggai 2:4

"...be strong, all ye people of the land saith the Lord, and work; for I am with you, saith the Lord of hosts:"

Be strong in the Lord
And in the power of his might
Knowing as you work in his field
Your enemy will soon take flight

For you know the Lord is with you
And he will see you through
Blessing the work of your hands
Blessing all you say and do

Apples of Gold

March 24

Zechariah 4:6

"…Not by might, nor by power, but by my spirit, saith the Lord of hosts."

It will not be our power
It will not be our might
That causes us to win the war
Or causes us to win the fight

It will be his precious Spirit
That gives us the grace
To overcome our enemy
And look him in the face

Apples of Gold

March 25

Zechariah 4:10

**"For who hath despised the day
of small things?..."**

Small stones slew a giant
A small prayer brought down fire
Don't despise the small things
For Satan is a liar

Satan tries to belittle
And make you small in your own eyes
But little is much when God is in it
So don't believe his lies

Apples of Gold

March 26

Zephaniah 2:3

"Seek the Lord, all ye meek of the earth, which have wrought his judgment; seek righteousness, seek meekness; it may be ye shall be hid in the day of the Lord's anger."

Seek for yourself a refuge
A place where you can go
To escape the wrath to come
While living here below

You won't believe the power
That is found in meekness
Even though the world
May see it as weakness

Apples of Gold

March 27

Zechariah 2:8

"...he that toucheth you toucheth the apple of his eye."

When the world attacks
A Christian who is true
They are saying to God
I'm fighting with you

We are his children
The apple of his eye
To believe anything less
Is to believe a lie

Apples of Gold

March 28

Malachi 3:6-7

"For I am the Lord, I change not;
therefore you sons of Jacob are not
consumed...Return unto me,
and I will return unto you,
saith the Lord of hosts..."

The Lord changes not
And ever He is calling
His wayward sons and daughters
To keep them from falling

Come home, the clouds are gathering
I want you by my side
You need to be near me
So under my wings, you can hide

Apples of Gold

March 29

Matthew 4:4

"...It is written, Man shall not live by bread alone, but by every word that proceedeth out of the mouth of God."

Sometimes the bread of this world
Leaves us empty and alone
There is a place of refuge
At the Fathers throne

We need the words of Jesus
To make it through this life
To lift us up on high
Above the fighting and strife

Apples of Gold

March 30

Matthew 10:36

"And a man's foes shall be they of his own household."

Sometimes it's a stranger
Sometimes it's a friend
The enemy can use almost anyone
Even those on whom we depend

So keep your eyes on Jesus
The one who knows the way
For then on the right path
You will be sure to stay

Apples of Gold

March 31

Matthew 11:28-30

"Come unto me, all ye that labour and are heavy laden, and I will give you rest. Take my yoke upon you, and learn of me; for I am meek and lowly in heart: and ye shall find rest unto your souls. For my yoke is easy, and my burden is light."

Are you heavy laden
Do you need some rest
Here's an invitation
To come and be his guest

He will lift your burden
Give you back your peace
If to the Lord
Your life, you will release

Apples of Gold

April 1

Matthew 13:49

"So shall it be at the end of the world; the angels shall come forth, and sever the wicked from among the just"

Do not fret yourself
Over what the wicked do
God has not left this task
In the hands of me and you

For at the very end
The angels will take charge
And do this simple work
Which to us seemed so large

Apples of Gold

April 2

Mark 2:17

"… They that are whole have no need of the physician, but they that are sick; I came not to call the righteous, but sinners to repentance."

The Lord came for sinners
To heal and forgive
To give them a reason
And purpose to live

He loves them so dearly
That he gave up his son
And would have done so
To save even one

Apples of Gold

April 3

Mark 4:9

"...He that hath ears to hear,
let him hear."

Will you hear his voice
Will you hear him calling
Will you believe
He came to keep you from falling

He will not force you
But he begs you please
Come to my throne
And fall to your knees

Apples of Gold

April 4

Mark 4:41

"And they feared exceedingly,
and said one to another, What manner of
man is this, that even the wind and
the sea obey him?"

He commands the wind and seas
And him they obey
Will you not come
To your creator today

He longs to have you near him
To make your hurts subside
And have you close forever
And with you ever abide

Apples of Gold

April 5

Mark 6:31

"Come ye yourselves apart into a desert place, and rest a while;..."

There is a place, alone with him
Where secrets are revealed
Where all heaven and earth must stand
at bay
For he will be thy shield

Not storm or tempest can touch thee there
For it's a place of grace and power
Where the maker of heaven and earth
Spends with you one hour

Apples of Gold

April 6

Mark 7:6

"Well hath Esaias prophesied of you hypocrites, as it is written This people honoureth me with their lips, but their heart is far from me."

Oh, how many claim the name
That really do not know him
They profess to walk with God
But God does not know them

They must repent
And turn around
Or they will find themselves
On sinking ground

Apples of Gold

April 7

Mark 7:37

"...He hath done all things well..."

When things make no sense
And reasons, we can't tell
We can remember one thing
He hath done all things well

And whether we understand it
While here on earth below
One day the veil will lift
And all these things we'll know

Apples of Gold

April 8

Mark 9:23

"Jesus said unto him, If thou canst believe, all things are possible to him that believeth."

If you can believe
All things are possible
The Lord will do for you
What men say is impossible

He is able to do above
What you can think or ask
And for him, this act of power
Is but a small task

Apples of Gold

April 9

2 Kings 1:3

"But the angel of the Lord said to Elijah the Tishbite, Arise, go up to meet the messengers of the king of Samaria, and say unto them, Is it not because there is not a God in Israel, that you go to enquire of Baal-zebub the god of Ekron?"

Seek not supernatural help
From any other being
But the God of Israel
Who is all knowing and all seeing

Seeking any other
Is not the thing to do
For in the end
The cost will be too much for me and you

Apples of Gold

April 10

2 Kings 12:5

"Let the priests take it to them, every man of his acquaintance; and let them repair the breaches of the house, wheresoever any breach shall be found."

Shall we look for breaches
In our life today
That keep us from the Lord
And cause us to stray

In order to return to God
The breaches we must repair
And then our loving Father
Will hear and answer prayer

Apples of Gold

April 11

2 Kings 17:9

"And the children of Israel did secretly those things that were not right against the Lord their God, and they built them high places in all their cities, from the tower of the watchmen to the fenced city"

You cannot sin in secret
Against an omnipotent God
He's sees everything you do
And knows everywhere you trod

He knows your rising up
And sees your sitting down
He longs to give a smile
In exchange for that frown

Apples of Gold

April 12

2 Kings 17:33

"They feared the Lord, and served their own gods, after the manner of the nations whom they carried away from thence."

Can it be possible, to fear the Lord
And still to serve another
To seek to serve our flesh
And still call Jesus brother

Yes, I'm afraid it's possible
And more common than we know
To profess the name of Jesus
And still serve Satan, our foe

Apples of Gold

April 13

2 Kings 17:39

"But the Lord your God ye shall fear; and he shall deliver you out of the hand of all your enemies."

When you fear the Lord
Nothing else need you fear
For he will lead and guide you
And keep you, Oh, so near

He will not forsake you
Nor ever let you down
He will smile upon you
Though the world may frown

Apples of Gold

April 14

2 Kings 19:22

"Whom hast thou reproached and blasphemed? And against whom hast thou exalted thy voice, and lifted up thine eyes on high? Even against the Holy One of Israel."

To speak against the Lord
Tis not very wise
For all you say and do
Is within the gaze of his eyes

He knows all your thoughts
He has seen all your pain
He longs to comfort you
And wash away the stain

Apples of Gold

April 15

1 Chronicles 4:10

"And Jabez called on the God of Israel, saying, Oh that thou wouldest bless me indeed, and enlarge my coast, and that thine hand might be with me, and that thou wouldest keep me from evil, that it may not grieve me! And God granted him that which he requested."

God answers prayer
Every day and every night
So neglect not to pray
So that for you he will fight

He can bless you indeed
If his ways you seek
And change your situation
So it shall not be so bleak

Apples of Gold

April 16

1 Corinthians 6:20

"For ye are bought with a price: therefore glorify God in your body, and in your spirit, which are God's"

You are not your own
You've been bought with a price
So glorify the Lord
And forsake every vice

He owns you ever so totally
Your body and your spirit
And only when we seek his face
His blessings do we merit

Apples of Gold

April 17

1 Corinthians 7:23

**"Ye are bought with a price;
be not ye the servants of men."**

Do not fear mere man
Who can neither save nor forgive
But fear your God in heaven
Who causes you to live

He gave you breath and bought you back
From Satan here below
All his love and all his blessings
He longs for you to know

Apples of Gold

April 18

1 Corinthians 11:3

"But I would have you know, that the head of every man is Christ; and the head of the woman is the man; and the head of Christ is God."

God's order is so perfect
God's order is so right
If we honor his order
He will lead us through the night

He wrote the owners manual
Of life and death and grace
And if we follow his instructions
One day we'll see his face

Apples of Gold

April 19

1 Corinthians 15:58

"Therefore, my beloved brethren,
be ye steadfast, unmoveable, always
abounding in the work of the Lord,
forasmuch as you know that your labor
is not in vain in the Lord."

Some days it seems so futile
To toil and serve the Lord
Other days it's easy
When with him, we're in one accord

But we can know, that when we serve him
Our labor is not in vain
For our rewards shall be many
Worth every struggle, worth ever pain

Apples of Gold

April 20

1 Corinthians 16:9

"For a great door and effectual is opened unto me, and there are many adversaries."

When the Lord opens a door
The adversaries may be on every side
But he will help you defeat each one
If in him you will abide

For there is no weapon formed against you
That ever shall avail
For the Lord will send you angels
More than tongue can tell

Apples of Gold

April 21

2 Corinthians 3:5-6

"Not that we are sufficient of ourselves to think any thing as of ourselves; but our sufficiency is of God; Who also hath made us able ministers of the new testament; not of the letter, but of the spirit: for the letter killeth, but the spirit giveth live."

Not rules not regulations
Not traditions of men
Can make you any better
Or keep you from your sins

It's the Holy Spirit in you
That has the power to save
Make you an over comer
And raise you from the grave

Apples of Gold

April 22

2 Corinthians 4:8-9

"We are troubled on every side, yet not distressed; we are perplexed, but not in despair; Persecuted, but not forsaken; cast down, but not destroyed;"

Paul had trouble on every side
But God did not forsake him
He was persecuted but not destroyed
And although things looked grim

He knew in whom he had believed
And knew he would see him through
He would see him through his darkest day
And one day make all things new

Apples of Gold

April 23

2 Corinthians 4:13

"We having the same spirit of faith, according as it is written, I believed, and therefore have I spoken; we also believe, and therefore speak;"

What we believe speaks volumes
It's what we say and do
It's what makes us who we are
And it's what sees us through

So be careful what you believe
Make sure you believe no lie
It will determine where you spend eternity
And what happens when you die

Apples of Gold

April 24

2 Corinthians 5:17

"Therefore if any man be in Christ, he is a new creature; old things are passed away; behold, all things are become new."

Do you want a new start
Do you want a new life
Because of what Jesus did
You can be delivered from strife

He is very able
To make all things new
And give a second chance
To even me and you

Apples of Gold

April 25

2 Corinthians 10:3

"For though we walk in the flesh, we do not war after the flesh:"

For though we walk in the flesh
Our enemy works in the spirit realm
And only can be defeated
By the blood of the Lamb

So when you're tired of fighting him
All on your own
Look to Jesus Christ
And look to him alone

Apples of Gold

April 26

2 Corinthians 10:4

"(For the weapons of our warfare are not carnal, but mighty through God to the pulling down of strong holds;)"

We have weapons that are not of this world
But are powerful indeed
And they will work for us
When his blood we can plead

To have this blood applied
Go to John 3:16
And when you understand this verse
You will know what I mean

Apples of Gold

April 27

2 Corinthians 11:14-15

"And no marvel; for Satan himself is transformed into and angel of light. Therefore it is no great thing if his ministers also be transformed as the ministers of righteousness; whose end shall be according to their works."

If you see evil in pulpits
Do not be surprised
For they have been put there by Satan
To do and spread his lies

The Lord says not to marvel
For Satan himself appears as light
It's just another sign
We're entering the darkest night

Apples of Gold

April 28

Galatians 1:9

**"As we said before, so say I now again,
If any man preach any other gospel unto
you than that ye have received,
let him be accursed."**

It's time to learn the truth
Or we shall believe a lie
And be ever so shocked
When it's our time to die

The night is surely coming
So work while it is day
For it will not be much longer
Till the church will be caught away

Apples of Gold

April 29

Galatians 3:13

"Christ hath redeemed us from the curse of the law, being made a curse for us: for it is written, Cursed is every one that hangeth on a tree:"

Jesus became a curse
So we could live free
He died an awful death
To save you and me

But he rose again
On the third day
So we could follow him to heaven
Yes, he and he alone made the way

Apples of Gold

April 30

Psalms 105:28

"He sent darkness, and make it dark; and they rebelled not against his word."

Darkness came to Moses and Aaron
But they still obeyed the Lord
And knew that with their God
They must stay in one accord

For when the darkness comes
And Satan tries to make you fear
Just know that though you can't see Jesus
He is still ever so near

Apples of Gold

May 1

Proverbs 15:27

"He that is greedy of gain troubleth his own house;..."

When we are greedy
Lusting after money
Tis then we will be driven
Out of the land of milk and honey

So let us be content
With what the Lord shall give
Knowing in his presence
We shall ever live

Apples of Gold

May 2

John 13:7

"Jesus answered and said unto him, What I do thou knowest not now; but thou shalt know hereafter."

Sometimes we must wait
In order to understand
What the Lord is doing
With his mighty hand

His ways are far above us
Beyond our finding out
But when we see the end result
We will surely want to shout

Apples of Gold

May 3

John 12:43

"For they loved the praise of men more than the praise of God."

It is a dangerous thing
When we love the praise of men
And if left unchecked
Can lead us into sin

So look for your approval
From your Father above
For we can trust his opinion
Knowing it comes from a heart of love

Apples of Gold

May 4

Acts 5:41

"And they departed from the presence of the council, rejoicing that they were counted worthy to suffer shame for his name."

When we can rejoice in suffering
Like the disciples of old
We will then know our faith
Is nearing pure gold

So let us seek a closer walk
As we see the hour darken
So that in our time of need
To his voice we will hearken

Apples of Gold

May 5

Romans 4:20-21

"He staggered not at the promise of God through unbelief; but was strong in faith, giving glory to God; And being fully persuaded that, what he had promised, he was able also to perform."

Abraham he staggered not
At the precious promise
He did not allow himself
To be like doubting Thomas

So let us follow Abraham's lead
And believe that God is able
To fulfill every promise
And before our enemies, spread a table

Apples of Gold

May 6

Romans 5:8

"But God commendeth his love toward us, in that, while we were yet sinners, Christ died for us."

The Lord waited not for you to be perfect
Nor to get everything right
He sent his Son to die for you
In the darkest, cruelest night

Yes, he died for us
While we we're all still sinners
To save us from Satan's wrath
And cause us to be winners

Apples of Gold

May 7

Jeremiah 1:8

"Be not afraid of their faces: for I am with thee to deliver thee, saith the Lord."

When we preach the truth
Some faces may frown
But if we remain steadfast
We shall receive a crown

So don't ever compromise
The truth of the Bible
For only those with sound doctrine
Can have true revival

Apples of Gold

May 8

Jeremiah 1:17

"Thou therefore gird up thy loins, and arise, and speak unto them all that I command thee: be not dismayed at their faces, lest I confound thee before them."

It's better to speak
What the Lord commands
Than to speak
To please mere man

So speak the truth in boldness
Rightly dividing the word
So that all the truth of God
Can be easily seen and heard

Apples of Gold

May 9

Luke 18:1

"And he spake a parable unto them to this end that men ought always to pray, and not to faint:"

Be ever so prayerful
As you pass through your day
So that God in His mercy
Can show you the way

Let not your faith faint
Nor your heart be full of trouble
For when your breakthrough comes
Your blessings will be double

Apples of Gold

May 10

Romans 16:17

"Now I beseech you, brethren, mark them which cause division and offences contrary to the doctrine which ye have learned; and avoid them."

There has always been
And there will always be
Those that cause division
Haunting you and me

The Lord says we should mark them
And avoid them at all cost
So that our love for the brethren
Shall not be forever lost

Apples of Gold

May 11

Colossians 2:8

"Beware lest any man spoil you through philosophy and vain deceit, after the tradition of men, after the rudiments of the world, and not after Christ."

Oh, the wise philosophers
They think themselves quite smart
And would that they could deceive you
Make you, from your Savior depart

So hold fast to the scriptures
That against Him, you might not sin
And follow not the way of the world
Nor the traditions of men

Apples of Gold

May 12

1Timothy 4:1

"Now the Spirit speaketh expressly, that in the latter times some shall depart from the faith, giving heed to seducing spirits, and doctrines of devils."

All that glitters
Surely is not gold
For devils can do miracles
In Exodus we're told

For when Moses and Aaron
Threw down their rod
The magicians did the same
When Pharaoh gave the nod

Apples of Gold

May 13

1Timothy 6:10

"For the love of money is the root of all evil: which while some coveted after, they have erred from the faith, and pierced themselves through with many sorrows."

Oh, the love of money
What sorrows that can bring
When we put our trust
In such a fleeting thing

So if we err from the faith
While coveting after money
We may never see the land
That flows with milk and honey

Apples of Gold

May 14

Ezekiel 17:24

"And all the trees of the field shall know that I the Lord have brought down the high tree, have exalted the low tree, have dried up the green tree, and have made the dry tree to flourish: I the Lord have spoken and have done it."

Oh, how things can change
When the Lord moves things around
He puts down the high and lifts up the low
Without even making a sound

He can dry up the green tree
And make the dry to flourish
Set down the high and mighty
And the lowly He will nourish

Apples of Gold

May 15

Amos 3:7

"Surely the Lord God will do nothing, but he revealeth his secret unto his servants the prophets."

What kind of a God
Would whisper in our ear
Allow us to see
Allow us to hear

The wonders of His miracles
The works of His hands
And reveal such things
To simple mortal man

Apples of Gold

May 16

Amos 5:4

"For thus saith the Lord unto the house of Israel, Seek ye me, and ye shall live."

The hour is getting late
It's time to seek His face
For soon and very soon
Sound doctrine, will have no place

Seek the Lord
While He may be found
Or you will find yourself
On very shaky ground

Apples of Gold

May 17

Amos 8:17

"Behold, the days come, saith the Lord, that I will send a famine in the land, not a famine of bread, nor a thirst for water, but of hearing the words of the Lord;"

There's coming a famine
Of that I am sure
When it will be hard to find
Words that are holy and pure

So store them up now
Hide them in your heart
So when the famine comes
From Him you'll not depart

Apples of Gold

May 18

Jonah 1:9

"And he said unto them, I am an Hebrew; and I fear the Lord, the God of heaven, which hath made the sea and the dry land."

The fear of the Lord
Is what we need
In these last days
It's wisdom indeed

For He is the God of heaven
The one who made the sea
And then turned His attention
To making you and me

Apples of Gold

May 19

Jonah 2:7

"When my soul fainted within me
I remembered the Lord:
and my prayer came in unto thee,
into thine holy temple."

When my soul had fainted
And there was no hope for me
It was then that you picked me up
And placed me on your knee

You told me that you loved me
No matter what I had done
And that because of your victory
I now had won

Apples of Gold

May 20

John 15:15

"Henceforth I call you not servants; for the servant knoweth not what his lord doeth: but I have called you friends; for all things that I have heard of my Father I have made known unto you."

Can you even imagine
That God can call you friend
And heal all your wounds
And your broken heart, mend

Well it's true He can do it
Because He did it for me
And no respecter of persons
Will He ever be

Apples of Gold

May 21

Deuteronomy 8:3

"And he humbled thee,
and suffered thee to hunger,
and fed thee with manna, which thou
knewest not, neither did thy fathers
know; that he might make thee know that
man doth not live by bread only, but by
every word that proceedeth out of the
mouth of the Lord doth man live."

Sometimes we must be humbled
Caused to hunger and thirst
So we will know what is important
And remember to put God first

Get our eyes off the temporal
And on His word alone
Lift our gaze off this world
And focus it on the throne

Apples of Gold

May 22

Ecclesiastes 5:5-6

"Better is it that thou shouldest not vow, than that thou shouldest vow and not pay. Suffer not thy mouth to cause thy flesh to sin; neither say thou before the angel, that it was an error: wherefore should God be angry at thy voice, and destroy the work of thine hands?"

Modern day prophets
Say just make a vow
If you cannot pay
God will not judge you now

But scripture says
That unto us that is sin
So we can listen to God
Or we can listen to men

Apples of Gold

May 23

Isaiah 42:19-20

"Who is blind, but my servant? Or deaf, as my messenger that I sent? Who is blind as he that is perfect, and blind as the Lord's servant? Seeing many things, but thou observest not; opening the ears, but he heareth not."

When He places something
Ever before our eyes
We should be like Moses
And there turn aside

Turn aside to see
What the Lord has to say
And be ever so mindful
Of what He's telling you today

Apples of Gold

May 24

Ezekiel 16:49

"Behold, this was the iniquity of thy sister Sodom, pride, fullness of bread, and abundance of idleness was in her and in her daughters, neither did she strengthen the hand of the poor and needy."

When we're full of pride
And we have plenty of bread
It's not long before our prosperity
Can go to our head

So be careful, very careful
How you look at the poor
For riches can make themselves wings
And fly away for sure

Apples of Gold

May 25ᵗ

Mark 1:17

"And Jesus said unto them,
Come ye after me, and I will make you
to become fishers of men."

There is a job more noble
Than any we can do
It's catching the souls of men
And for that He can use me and you

So let us submit our members
And all that we can say
To the one that will say well done
On that great and glorious day

Apples of Gold

May 26

Luke 3:10-11

"And the people asked him, saying, What shall we do then? He answereth and saith unto them, He that hath two coats, let him impart to him that hath none; and he that hath meat, let him do likewise."

So when you see the needy
Turn not your face away
But give them of your substance
Knowing God, He will repay

For when you give to the needy
You are giving God a loan
He will be no mans debtor
He will forget not the seeds you've sown

Apples of Gold

May 27

Acts 12:11

"And when Peter was come to himself, he said, Now I know of a surety, that the Lord hath sent his angel, and hath delivered me out of the hand of Herod, and from all the expectation of the people of the Jews."

Ever been in a situation
Where there seemed to be no way out
But then the Lord delivered
And made you want to shout

Take the time to thank Him
For what He's already done
And know the battle you're in right now
Has already been won

Apples of Gold

May 28

John 7:7

"The world cannot hate you; but me it hateth, because I testify of it, that the works thereof are evil."

Oh, how the world hates Jesus
The things He says and does
But He is still the one to come
The one who is and the one who was

His life testifies how evil
The world it is today
And shows all the sinners
They are going the wrong way

Apples of Gold

May 29

John 13:34-35

"A new commandment I give unto you, That ye love one another; as I have loved you, that ye also love one another. By this shall all men know that ye are my disciples, if you have love one to another."

It's not rules and regulations
That makes the world take notice
It is the love for our brothers and sisters
As the Lord has shown us

So if we would be like Jesus
We must love one another
And serve the living God
And serve no other

Apples of Gold

May 30

Romans 3:23

"For all have sinned, and come short of the glory of God."

All have missed the mark
And fallen short of God's glory
We're all in this together
And all have similar stories

But the good news is
We can all be forgiven
If we look to the Lord
The maker of earth and heaven

Apples of Gold

May 31

Romans 8:31

**"What shall we then say to these things?
If God be for us, who can be against us?"**

If we are in the ark
Covered in the blood
Our enemies will surely fall
Just like those in the flood

God will not suffer,
Us to be wronged forever
But will repay justly
For He is Oh so clever

Apples of Gold

June 1

Romans 10:9

"That if thou shalt confess with thy mouth the Lord Jesus, and shalt believe in thine heart that God hath raised him from the dead, thou shalt be saved."

Confess and believe
Jesus was raised from the dead
And the blessings of God
Shall ever rest upon thine head

For with the mouth we make confession
And with the heart we believe
Therefore our sins are forgiven
And all our quilt is relieved

Apples of Gold

June 2

Romans 10:13

"For whosoever shall call upon the name of the Lord shall be saved."

Whosoever shall call
On the name of the Lord
Shall find their place in heaven
And receive their reward

But those who turn away
From the grace of God
Shall never see His glory
And never with Him trod

Apples of Gold

June 3

Romans 12:1

"I beseech you therefore, brethren, by the mercies of God, that ye present your bodies a living sacrifice, holy, acceptable unto God, which is your reasonable service."

If you belong to Jesus
Have given Him your life
Then serve Him with gladness
While avoiding this world's strife

It is your reasonable service
To give your very best
And once you have done this
On His promises you can rest

Apples of Gold

June 4

Galatians 1:9

"As we said before, so say I now again,
If any man preach any other gospel
unto you than that ye have received
let him be accursed."

There is another gospel
Being preached throughout the land
That says, with other religions
We should walk hand in hand

But Jesus says, of a truth
There is but one way
To enter into the kingdom
And found not guilty on that day

Apples of Gold

June 5

2 Thessalonians 1:6

"Seeing it is a righteous thing with God to recompense tribulation to them that trouble you:"

We are not to repay
Our enemies here below
But rest assured my brothers
Their payment, God will bestow

At the perfect time
At the perfect hour
The Lord will recompense
Through His great power

Apples of Gold

June 6

1ˢᵗ Peter 4:17

"For the time is come that judgment must begin at the house of God: and if it first begin at us, what shall the end be of them that obey not the gospel of God?"

Judgment is coming
For sinner and saint
But if we know Jesus
It will not make us faint

We have a refuge
The sinner does not know
And on that dreadful day
We have a safe place to go

Apples of Gold

June 7

Revelation 2:11

"He that hath an ear, let him hear what the Spirit saith unto the churches; He that overcometh shall not be hurt of the second death."

Listen to the Lord
If He's speaking to you
And then the second death
You will not have to go through

The second death consists
Of eternal separation
From all light and love
Into a horrible destination

Apples of Gold

June 8

Psalms 3:6

"I will not be afraid of ten thousands of people that have set themselves against me round about."

If God is with you
He can keep you from fear
If thousands gather against you
From far and near

For as Jesus told Pilate
Against me you could have no power
Were it not given to you by my father
For this very hour

Apples of Gold

June 9

Leviticus 18:22

"Thou shalt not lie with mankind, as with womankind: it is abomination."

God says it's an abomination
For man to lie with man
I don't know what part of this
The liberals don't understand

They say it is their right
To do as they please
But there is coming a day
When they will be on their knees

Apples of Gold

June 10

Ezekiel 3:17

"Son of man, I have made thee a watchman unto the house of Israel: therefore hear the word at my mouth, and give them warning from me."

If we don't give them warning
Their blood shall be on our hands
According to the scripture
According to His commands

So be very careful
Whom you neglect to tell
You would not want to be
The reason they are in Hell

Apples of Gold

June 11

Genesis 26:22

"...For now the Lord hath made room for us, and we shall be fruitful in the land."

Isaac fought over many wells
But then there came a day
When God said this one's yours
No matter what they say

Rest assured God has a place for you
Even though it's been a long fight
He will give you peace from your enemies
Through His great power and might

Apples of Gold

June 12

Genesis 31:16

"...Whatsoever God hath said unto thee, do."

When God gives you direction
Don't question and rebel
Just be sure if you follow instruction
Your circumstances will turn out well

Turn not to the left
Turn not to the right
For He's with you in the battle
He's with you in the fight

Apples of Gold

June 13

2 Kings 2:21

"...I have healed these waters;
there shall not be from thence any more
death or barren land."

When the Lord has healed your waters
And delivered you from barren land
What a time for rejoicing
At the work of his hand

You can now reap
From the things you have sown
And claim the promises
For your very own

Apples of Gold

June 14

Ezekiel 13:3

"Thus saith the Lord God; Woe unto the foolish prophets, that follow their own spirit, and have seen nothing!"

Some of them have a vision
Some have a word
Some of them are real
Others from God, have not heard

In order to know the difference
We must hide the word in our heart
So that from the TRUE God
We will know not to depart

Apples of Gold

June 15

Mark 4:40

"And he said unto them, Why are ye so fearful? How is it that ye have no faith?"

We fear what will men will do
We forget they have no power
And can do nothing to us
For even a single hour

Lest it be given them
By the God of all might
Who could let them trouble us
But will never let them win the fight

Apples of Gold

June 16

Luke 9:1

"Then He called his twelve disciples
together, and gave them power
and authority over all devils,
and to cure diseases."

Let us never forget

We have power over all devils

And remember with joy

We can defeat him on all levels

He's like a barking dog

Tied to a stake

He can make a lot of noise

But only what we give him, can he take

Apples of Gold

June 17

Galatians 4:29

"But as then he that was born after the flesh persecuted him that was born after the Spirit, even so it is now."

There are ministries born of the flesh
And ministries born of the Spirit
The Lord will show you the difference
If the still small voice, you can hear it

But if you rely on your senses
What you see and what you hear
You could be led astray
And that we all should fear

Apples of Gold

June 18

1 Samuel 15:23

"For rebellion is as the sin of witchcraft, and stubbornness is as iniquity and idolatry…"

You might as well practice witchcraft
If in rebellion you dwell
For both of them alike
Will surely send you to hell

And stubbornness is no better
The Bible says it is sin
So if you find yourself being stubborn
You will have to repent again

Apples of Gold

June 19

1 Samuel 24:12

"The Lord judge between me and thee, and the Lord avenge me of thee: but mine hand shall not be upon thee."

If you wrong me
I will not take revenge
But pray to God in heaven
To take up my cause and avenge

And at the proper time
He will judge between me and thee
He will do the right thing
I'm sure you will agree

Apples of Gold

June 20

1 Chronicles 16:11

"Seek the Lord and his strength, seek his face continually."

Seek the Lord with all your heart
While He may be found
So that when trouble comes
You'll be on solid ground

Seek His face continually
Daily in prayer
And it won't be long until
You'll find He meets you there

Apples of Gold

June 21

Psalms 30:11

"Thou hast turned for me my mourning into dancing:"

There is a time for dancing
There is a time to mourn
Sometimes we feed on manna
Sometimes we feed on corn

Regardless of our circumstance
Regardless of our need
He knows how to feed us
And He knows where to lead

Apples of Gold

June 22

Psalms 55:21

"The words of his mouth were smoother than butter, but war was in his heart: his words were softer than oil, yet were they drawn swords."

Oh for discernment
To tell friend from foe
Some can talk the talk
But the walk, they may not know

Jesus committed to no man
For He saw the heart
Knew when to draw close
And knew when to depart

Apples of Gold

June 23

Psalms 119:67

"Before I was afflicted I went astray:
but now have I kept thy word."

Before I was afflicted
I easily went astray
But now I've learned
To love Him more everyday

I have learned that the word
Will keep me near the master
And cause me to get the victory
Oh, so much faster

Apples of Gold

June 24

Psalms 119:165

"Great peace have they which love they law: and nothing shall offend them."

Do we love thy law
Do we have great peace
Or are we easily offended
Does our happiness easily cease

We should be offended at nothing
Knowing God has our back
Our peace should be great
And our joy shall not lack

Apples of Gold

June 25

Numbers 12:2

"And they said, Hath the Lord indeed spoken only by Moses? Hath he not spoken also by us? And the Lord heard it."

When we talk about our brother
As Miriam thought to do
Our father in heaven hears us
And sees who we are talking to

He dealt with these two siblings
For stabbing Moses in the back
He dealt with them severely
And got them back on track

Apples of Gold

June 26

1 Chronicles 17:23

"Therefore now, Lord, let the thing that thou hast spoken concerning thy servant and concerning his house be established for ever, and do as thou hast said."

If from the Lord, you have a promise
To Him you can pray it back
And be sure to get you answer
And have to suffer no lack

If you have not received a promise
Stay in the word day and night
And He will surely speak to you
Make all your wrong things right

Apples of Gold

June 27

1 Corinthians 16:9

"For a great door and effectual is opened unto me, and there are many adversaries."

When the Lord opens your door of opportunity
Many foes may lay at your feet
But the Lord will make a way for you
When the adversary you meet

For greater is He that is in me
Than he that is in the world
And God will give us the victory
If our cares on Him, we have hurled

Apples of Gold

June 28

1 Corinthians 15:58

"Therefore, my beloved brethren, be ye steadfast, unmovable, always abounding in the work of the Lord, forasmuch as ye know that your labour is not in vain in the Lord."

If you are laboring for the Lord
The fruit, one day you will reap
No matter how barren it looks
No matter how bleak

For He has promised
Our labour is not in vain
And if we don't give up
The victory we will surely gain

Apples of Gold

June 29

2Timothy 3:13

"But evil men and seducers shall wax worse and worse, deceiving, and being deceived."

Evil men and seducers
We have with us today
And we will have them when
the trumpet sounds
And we're all caught away

They are going to get worse
According to the scripture
God's giving us fair warning
He's painting us a picture

Apples of Gold

June 30

James 4:17

"Therefore to him that knoweth to do good, and doeth it not, to him it is sin."

We can't say we didn't know
The difference between right and wrong
That won't work with the father
And He won't stand for that for long

So if you know what's right
And if you do it not
You may be close to judgment
Like our brother Lot

Apples of Gold

July 1

2 Kings 1:3

"But the angel of the Lord said to Elijah the Tishbite, Arise, go up to meet the messengers of the king of Samaria, and say unto them, Is it not because there is not a God in Israel, that ye go to enquire of Baal-zebub the god of Ekron?"

The King of Samaria sent his men
To seek counsel of another god
That's when the God of Israel
Gave Elijah the nod

To go and intercept them
And let them know the dangers
Of seeking other gods
The gods of foreign strangers

Apples of Gold

July 2

Ezekiel 33:33

"And when this cometh to pass, (lo, it will come,) then shall they know that a prophet hath been among them."

The Lord may speak through you
Use your lowly voice
And give the ones you speak to
The right to make their choice

But whether they heed you or not
Eventually they will know
That a prophet has been among them
For God, the truth to them will show

Apples of Gold

July 3

Matthew 3:17-4:1

"And lo a voice from heaven, saying. This is my beloved Son, in whom I am well pleased. Then was Jesus led up of the Spirit into the wilderness to be tempted of the devil."

Sometimes it's when we're at our best
That Satan tempts and tries
But rest assured that God in heaven
Hears our faintest cries

He will not leave you nor forsake you
No matter the wilderness you're in
For He has given us the blood
To make us victors over sin

Apples of Gold

July 4

Mathew 8:13

"....Go thy way; and as thou hast believed so be it done unto thee..."

As thou has believed
So be it unto thee
Satan can not steal our promise
And from us he must flee

So go your way believing
Every word the scripture proclaims
Knowing that believing God
Shall never be cause for shame

Apples of Gold

July 5

John 6:17

"...And it was now dark, and Jesus was not come to them..."

Sometimes the road gets dark
Before the Lord shows up
But keep trusting in Him daily
He will surely fill your cup

They say it's always darkest
Right before the dawn
So keep holding to His hand
And your fears will soon be gone

Apples of Gold

July 6

John 9:4

"I must work the works of him that sent me, while it is day: the night cometh, when no man can work."

Let us heed the scripture
And work while it is day
For I assure you brother
Night is on the way

I see the dark clouds gathering
They're coming closer still
It's time to work with all our might
And do the Fathers will

Apples of Gold

July 7

Acts 10:4

"Thy prayers and thine alms are come up for a memorial before God."

Our prayers are not wasted
Our alms are noticed too
They come before the Lord
As a memorial for me and you

That means He's taking notice
Of all the prayers we pray
And He will not fail to answer them
Could be this very day

Apples of Gold

July 8

Acts 10:31

"...Cornelius, thy prayer is heard, and thine alms are had in remembrance in the sight of God."

God in heaven, He hears our prayers
And remembers all our alms
He will send His angels to minister to us
And all our fears He calms

If He listened to Cornelius
He will certainly listen to us
For He's no respecter of persons
On that fact you can trust

Apples of Gold

July 9

Exodus 20:20

"...Fear not: for God is come to prove you, and that his fear may be before your faces, that ye sin not."

When circumstances scare you badly
You don't know where to turn
There is a real good possibility
God has a lesson for you to learn

He may have allowed this problem
To see what you will do
To see if the fear of God
Truly dwells in you!

Apples of Gold

July 10

Exodus 23:20

"Behold, I send an Angel before thee, to keep thee in the way, and bring thee into the place which I have prepared."

God has sent an Angel
To hold unto your hand
Until you reach your destination
In the promise land

He will lead and guide
Every step you take
So that the end result
Cannot be a mistake

Apples of Gold

July 11

Exodus 23:2

"Thou shalt not follow a multitude to do evil..."

Even though the crowd
Is sinning greatly now
To live a holy life
The Lord will show you how

We shall not follow the multitude
To do their awful deeds
For we do not want to reap
From sowing poisoned seeds

Apples of Gold

July 12

Exodus 23:30

"By little and little I will drive them out from before thee, until thou be increased, and inherit the land."

Your enemies may seem strong
Come against you in every way
But the Lord is driving them out
Little by little every day

One day we will look for them
And lo they will have vanished
And God will whisper in your ear
Your enemies, I have banished

Apples of Gold

July 13

Exodus 22:29

"Thou shalt not delay to offer the first of thy ripe fruits.."

To God we must offer
And our tithe pay
For this scripture says
We surely shall not delay

For He will reward us
If obedient we be
And the storehouse of heaven
He will open to you and me

Apples of Gold

July 14

Exodus 33:17

"...I will do this thing also that thou hast spoken: for thou hast found grace in my sight, and I know thee by name."

When we find grace
In the Lord's precious sight
We have tapped in
To His power and might

I can think of nothing
That I would rather hear
Than the Lord call my name
Because I've drawn so near

Apples of Gold

July 15

Psalms 126:6

"He that goeth forth and weepeth, bearing precious seed, shall doubtless come again with rejoicing, bringing his sheaves with him."

I have sown the seeds of sorrow
And watered them with my tears
And now the God of Israel
Has wiped away all my fears

There comes a time for reaping
The precious seed we have sown
Bringing in the sheaves
Knowing they're your very own

Apples of Gold

July 16

Ruth 2:10

"…Why have I found grace in thine eyes, that thou shouldest take knowledge of me, seeing I am a stranger?"

Why would God show us grace
When Him we do not know
Could it be to show His love
And how far He's willing to go

To call us into His little flock
And make our way secure
In the middle of this evil world
He will teach us to be holy and pure

Apples of Gold

July 17

Ruth 4:15

"And he shall be unto thee a restorer of thy life..."

When our life takes a turn
That we did not plan or know
God can surely make it right
And show us the way to go

Oh, what peace is found
When we put Him at the helm
For He can guide us safely through
The natural and spiritual realm

Apples of Gold

July 18

Isaiah 48:17

"Thus saith the Lord, thy Redeemer, the
Holy One of Israel; I am the Lord thy
God which teacheth thee to profit,
which leadeth thee by the way
that thou shouldest go."

It is not in man to know the way to go
So the scriptures say
We must rely on God alone
To show us the way

To live and love and manage life
And all that is therein
For only God's amazing grace
Gives us victory over sin

Apples of Gold

July 19

Isaiah 54:17

"No weapon that is formed against thee shall prosper; and every tongue that shall rise against thee in judgment thou shalt condemn. This is the heritage of the servants of the Lord, and their righteousness is of me, saith the Lord."

There will always be enemies
While we dwell here below
Thank God that our Father
Has broken the sword of our foe

Though the tongues are wagging
And the swords are flying fast
We will still be standing tall
When the smoke clears at last

Apples of Gold

July 20

Jeremiah 32:19

"Great in counsel, and mighty in work: for thine eyes are open upon all the ways of the sons of men: to give every one according to his ways, and according to the fruit of his doings:"

God is watching over
All the sons of men
To see the ones that will be turned away
And which ones He will gather in

So never think for a moment
Your deeds on earth are not known
That's why the Bible instructs us
We shall reap what we have sown

Apples of Gold

July 21

Daniel 5:20

"But when his heart was lifted up,
and his mind hardened in pride,
he was deposed from his kingly throne,
and they took his glory from him;"

When our heart is lifted up
And we are oh, so full of pride
It's then that we can be sure
Our foot is about to slide

For pride goeth before a fall
On this you can rely
For the word of God is never wrong
This we can't deny

Apples of Gold

July 22

Habakkuk 2:1

"I will stand upon my watch, and set me upon the tower, and will watch to see what he will say unto me..."

Oh, how wise the man
That sets upon his tower
And waits upon the word of God
For His instructions every hour

There's great peace in knowing
You have heard from the Father
For once you've heard His voice
Other voices can't thwart or bother

Apples of Gold

July 23

Mark 8:23

"And he took the blind man by hand,
and led him out of the town..."

It's oh so good to know
That when we are blind
To us the Lord
Will still be kind

He will come to where we are
And take us by the hand
Lead us to the center
Of His loving, perfect plan

Apples of Gold

July 24

Mark 7:33

"And he took him aside from
the multitude…"

Sometimes we must leave the multitude
To be alone with Him
To hear His still small voice
That we might not follow every whim

We must be grounded in the Lord
And in His precious word
So that when He speaks to us
His voice will surely be heard

Apples of Gold

July 25

Mark 9:23

"Jesus said unto him, If thou canst believe, all things are possible to him that believeth."

You must believe the Lord
No matter what you see
For believing is receiving
This word tells you and me

All things are possible
When in Him we trust
In order to receive His promise
Trust in Him you must

Apples of Gold

July 26

John 7:43

"So there was a division among the people because of him."

When you begin to follow Jesus
With all your heart and mind
Be ready for divisions
For some won't be very kind

Not all professing Christians
Really want His will
Some just try to bargain
And with Him make a deal

Apples of Gold

July 27

Acts 18:9-10

"Be not afraid, but speak, and hold not thy peace: For I am with thee, and no man shall set on thee to hurt thee: for I have much people in this city."

If God be for us
Whom shall we fear
No need to fear man
When help is oh, so near

When your trodding up your mountain
To your place of need
The provision is traveling
At the same speed!!

Apples of Gold

July 28

2 Corinthians 12:9

"Therefore I take pleasure in infirmities in reproaches, in necessities, in persecutions, in distresses for Christ's sake: for when I am weak, then am I strong."

When I am weak
Then I am strong
It sounds so impossible
It sounds so wrong

But since it is written
In God's holy word
I know it's a fact
I know whom I've heard

Apples of Gold

July 29

Galatians 1:9

**"As we said before, so say I now again,
If any man preach any other gospel
unto you than that ye have received,
let him be accursed."**

There's a new set of teaching
Skipping round the land
It's not been born of God
It's been born of man

They say we should not suffer
Never have any lack
They're quite a large group now
They call themselves saddleback

Apples of Gold

July 30

1st Samuel 10:7

"And let it be, when these signs are come unto thee, that thou do as occasion serve thee, for God is with thee."

When you know God is with you
You're safe in your endeavor
For nothing can come against God
Not now, no not ever

So when the Lord opens a door
Do not be scared to go through
For if He has lead you there
He will surely be with you

Apples of Gold

July 31

1 Samuel 11:9

"...Tomorrow, by that time the sun be hot, ye shall have help...."

What a sweet promise
From a wonderful Master
He will even send an Army
To keep us from disaster

So I will look to the Lord
And to His mighty hand
I won't trust in flesh
I won't turn to man

Apples of Gold

August 1

1 Samuel 12:16

"Now therefore stand and see this great thing, which the Lord will do before your eyes."

The Lord will do great things
Before your very eyes
Things you wouldn't believe
Could be so great and wise

So be prepared to rejoice
At what He's about to do
He's going to win the victory
For each of us, me and you

Apples of Gold

August 2

1 Samuel 12:21

"And turn ye not aside; for then should ye go after vain things, which cannot profit nor deliver; for they are vain."

From the mighty God
Do not turn aside
But rather be content
To, in Him abide

The world and all it's pleasures
Surely are in vain
And in the end my brother
They will cause you nothing but pain

Apples of Gold

August 3

1 Samuel 12:24

"Only fear the Lord, and serve him in truth with all your heart: for consider how great things he hath done for you."

Think about the Lord
And all He's done for you
And how He delivered
When you had done all you could do

He deserves our gratitude
More than we'll ever know
So let us give Him our love
And our affection, to Him show

Apples of Gold

August 4

1 Samuel 14:6

"...There is no restraint to the Lord
to save by many or by few."

It's nothing to the Lord
To save by many or by few
So commit all thy works to Him
All that you say and do

He will gladly save you
Pull you to His side
Place His feathers over you
Under His wings shall you abide

Apples of Gold

August 5

1 Samuel 15:22

"And Samuel said, Hath the Lord as great delight in burnt offerings and sacrifices, as in obeying the voice of the Lord? Behold, to obey is better than sacrifice, and to hearken than the fat of rams."

Even if you give unto the Lord
That's not all He requires
He wants us to obey Him
That we might not be found liars

So give Him your obedience
Give Him your best
That on that final day
You may enter into His rest

Apples of Gold

August 6

Haggai 2:4

"…be strong, all ye people of the land, saith the Lord, and work: for I am with you, saith the Lord of hosts:"

We must be strong
For our foes are many
But our weapons are mighty
And our provisions are plenty

So work for the Lord
While it is still called today
For darkness is coming
It's no time to play

Apples of Gold

August 7

Haggai 2:19

"Is the seed yet in the barn?
Yea, as yet the vine, and the fig tree,
and pomegranate, and the olive tree,
hath not brought forth: from this day,
will I bless you."

The seeds we've been sowing
Are about to spring up
Whatever we have sown
That shall fill our cup

If you've sown to the world
You shall reap from it destruction
If you've sown to the Lord
There shall be no corruption

Apples of Gold

August 8

Luke 9:62

"...No man having put his hand to the plough, and looking back, is fit for the kingdom of God."

Once you've started out
On the narrow way
There should be no looking back
No turning away

For as Peter said
Lord where would we go
For the way of truth and life
Only you, Jesus know

Apples of Gold

August 9

Acts 10:34

"Then Peter opened his mouth, and said, of a truth I perceive that God is no respecter of persons"

God is no respecter of persons
Whether rich or poor
His only concern
Is that we love Him more and more

So do not judge your brother
Based on worldly success
And don't compare them to yourself
Whether they have more or less

Apples of Gold

August 10

Romans 16:17

"Now I beseech you, brethren, mark them which cause divisions and offences contrary to the doctrine which ye have learned; and avoid them."

Would God tell you to avoid someone
Oh, yes indeed He would
For if they are causing division and strife
He knows they will do you no good

Not only should you avoid them
But mark them as well
For you surely don't want to follow them
Into the fiery pits of hell

Apples of Gold

August 11

1 Corinthians 1:18

"For the preaching of the cross is to them that perish foolishness, but unto us which are saved it is the power of God."

Some call preaching foolishness
And do not want to hear it
We need to pray for those
The conviction of the Holy Spirit

But to us which are saved
It is power indeed
To strengthen and protect us
In our hour of need

Apples of Gold

August 12

1 Corinthians 2:14

"But the natural man receiveth not the things of the Spirit of God; for they are foolishness unto him; neither can he know them, because they are spiritually discerned"

The natural man can't understand
The wonderful things of God
For they need the Holy Spirit
Through these truths to trod

You must be born again
To get this perfect vision
So for Jesus today
Please make your decision

Apples of Gold

August 13

Deuteronomy 15:7

"If there be among you a poor man of one of thy brethren within any of thy gates in thy land which the Lord thy God giveth thee, thou shalt not harden thine heart, nor shut thine hand from thy poor brother:"

Harden not thine heart
When you see the poor
The Lord will not be pleased
Nor bless you any more

For if you close your eyes
Or if you turn your back
It won't be long before
It's you that suffers lack

Apples of Gold

August 14

Psalms 7:15-16

"He made a pit, and digged it, and is fallen into the ditch which he made. His mischief shall return upon his own head, and his violent dealing shall come down upon his own pate."

The wicked come against us
From the left and the right
But God will cause them to fall
Through His great power and might

So the wicked should think twice
Before they come against a Christian
For little do they know
There on a self destructive mission

Apples of Gold

August 15th

Psalms 144:1

"Blessed be the Lord my strength, which teacheth my hands to war, and my fingers to fight:'

When we are born again
We are drafted into a fight
It's not all sunshine and roses
It's not all glitter and light

So we must learn to use these weapons
That we have been given
If we want to gain the victory
If we want to gain heaven!

Apples of Gold

August 16

Ezekiel 3:8-9

"Behold, I have made thy face strong against their faces, and thy forehead strong against their foreheads. As an adamant harder than flint have I made thy forehead: fear them not, neither be dismayed at their looks, though they be a rebellious house."

Fear not rebellious Israel
Though they scorn and stare
For the Lord is thy strength
And you are in his care

He's made your face strong
And your forehead too
And though they rise up against you
There's nothing they can do

Apples of Gold

August 17

Nahum 1:3

"The Lord is slow to anger, and great in power, and will not at all acquit the wicked: the Lord hath his way in the whirlwind and in the storm, and the clouds are the dust of his feet."

The Lord is slow to anger
And very great in power
You can trust Him with your life
Every day and every hour

But He can send the whirlwind
And the terrible storm
In order to protect His children
He will bare His mighty arm

Apples of Gold

August 18

John 3:17

**"John answered and said,
A man can receive nothing,
except it be given him from heaven."**

If you have a blessing
In your life here below
Don't question where it came from
For it was God who did bestow

He deserves all our thanks
He deserves all our love
For all that we have
Came from heaven above

Apples of Gold

August 19

Acts 13:2

"As they ministered to the Lord, and fasted, the Holy Ghost said, Separate me Barnabas and Saul for the work whereunto I have called them."

What different workers there would be
In the church today
If we followed this recipe
Before we set them on their way

But we look at the outward
Don't seek God for the heart
So the real men of God
Many times must depart

Apples of Gold

August 20

John 7:7

"The world cannot hate you; but me it hateth, because I testify of it, that the works thereof are evil."

Oh, how the world hates Jesus
Because of their evil deeds
But if they would just come to Him
They would find He would meet
all their needs

He longs to save them from their self
And from their evil too
Just as He has saved me
Just as He has saved you

Apples of Gold

August 21

John 6:17

"...And it was now dark, and Jesus was not come to them."

Sometimes it gets real dark
Before the Lord shows up
But He will be here just in time
To fill your empty cup

The full soul does not want Him
The hungry soul cries for more
Thus sometimes He must wait
Until our knees, they touch the floor

Apples of Gold

August 22

John 6:24

"When the people therefore saw that Jesus was not there, neither his disciples, they also took shipping, and came to Capernaum, seeking for Jesus."

Sometimes we seek for Jesus
And find He isn't there
That's the time to pack our bags
And look for Him elsewhere

For if we seek diligently
Him we shall surely find
And could even be surprised
He's in our hearts and in our mind

Apples of Gold

August 23

John 8:7

"...He that is without sin among you, let him first cast a stone at her."

Be slow to judge your brother
When a sin, he does commit
For a glance in the mirror
Might be where judgment fits

We've all fallen short
According to the word
So pray for your brother
Until your prayer is heard

Apples of Gold

August 24

John 8:10-11

"…Woman, where are those thine accusers? Hath no man condemned thee? She said. No man, Lord, And Jesus said unto her, Neither do I condemn thee: go, and sin no more."

The Lord came not to condemn
But to seek and to save
So let Him be your portion
And His word the thing you crave

Turn not to the left
Turn to the right
Seek Him every morning
Seek Him with all you might

Apples of Gold

August 25

John 8:32

"And ye shall know the truth, and the truth shall make you free."

When you know the truth
It will surely set you free
And bring you to a place
Where His glory you can see

So seek the truth as silver
Search for it as gold
For what you will get when you find it
The half has not been told

Apples of Gold

August 26

John 9:35

"...Doest thou believe on the Son of God?"

Do you believe
In the Son of God
If you answered yes
Golden streets, one day you will trod

He's waiting for your answer
So don't turn away
For the day of salvation
Yes, it is today

Apples of Gold

August 27

Zephaniah 1:12

"...I will search Jerusalem with candles,
and punish the men that are settled
on their lees:"

The Lord has come to search us
To see if we're content
Rich and in need of nothing
And all our efforts spent

We feel no need to fight
We feel no need to preach
For we are happy now
Thinking we are out of harms reach

Apples of Gold

August 28

Zephaniah 2:3

"Seek ye the Lord, all ye meek of the earth, which have wrought his judgment; seek righteousness, seek meekness, it may be ye shall be hid in the day of the Lord's anger."

We need to seek the Lord
To escape this worlds danger
And continue to seek him
To escape the Lord's anger

For there is coming a day
Where his wrath will be known
I thank God for the day
The escape hatch, I was shown

Apples of Gold

August 29

Zephaniah 1:14

"The great day of the Lord is near, it is near, and hasteth greatly…"

The day of the Lord is near
Nearer than it's ever been
We must seek forgiveness now
To get victory over sin

There will be no warning
Before the trumpet sounds
So be prepared my brother
For your feet to leave the ground

Apples of Gold

August 30

Zechariah 2:8

"...he that toucheth you toucheth the apples of his eye."

God holds you
As the apple of his eye
His great love and mercy
No man can deny

Those who do you wrong
Have wronged your heavenly Father
God will repay your enemies
And you won't have to bother

Apples of Gold

August 31

Zechariah 4:7

"Who art thou, O great mountain? Before Zerubbabel thou shalt become a plain"

Who is your mountain
What is his name
He shall before you
Truly become a plain

When God knocks them down
They won't be getting up
He will cause them to disappear
And with blessings, fill your cup

Apples of Gold

September 1

Zechariah 4:10

**"For who hath despised the day
of small things?"**

*Don't despise the day
Of your small beginnings
For God to give you
A great and glorious ending*

*So take those baby steps
All that you can take
For giant leaps of faith
They shall someday make*

Apples of Gold

September 2

Zechariah 11:17

"Woe to the idol shepherd that leaveth the flock! The sword shall be upon his arm, and upon his right eye; his arm shall be clean dried up, and his right eye shall be utterly darkened."

Woe to the idol shepherd
Who doesn't feed his flock
The Lord is not pleased
And the Lord shall not be mocked

So if you have been idol
Ask the Lord to forgive
And teach the hungry sheep
That if they look to the Lord, they shall live

Apples of Gold

September 3

Malachi 3:7

"Return unto me, and I will return unto you, saith the Lord of hosts…"

Have you been away from the Lord
For a long season
Just return to him and repent
You need not tell him the reason

For he knows all things
And longs to have you back
Wants to supply all your needs
So no good thing, you will lack

Apples of Gold

September 4

Malachi 3:8

"Will a man rob God? Yet ye have robbed me. But ye say wherein have we robbed thee? In tithes and offerings."

Have you ever robbed God
Then realized it was a mistake
And that from your own life
A blessing, you did take

So let us get our giving right
As soon as we can
So that our provisions and our blessings
Will be back on his master plan

Apples of Gold

September 5

Matthew 5:17

"Think not that I am come to destroy the law, or the prophets: I am not come to destroy, but to fulfil.

Jesus came not to destroy the law
Of that I am sure
No, he came to fulfill it
So we could live holy and pure

So don't dismiss the old
To welcome in the new
We must make our master Jesus
While keeping Moses in view

Apples of Gold

September 6

Matthew 6:24

"No man can serve two masters:
for either he will hate the one, and love
the other; or else he will hold to the one,
and despise the other. Ye cannot serve
God and mammon."

You can not serve God and mammon
No matter how hard you try
And you can't love one
While on the other you rely

You must make a choice
Will it be God or mammon
Money can fly away
But God can supply in famine

Apples of Gold

September 7

Matthew 7:13-14

"Enter ye in at the strait gate;
for wide is the gate, and broad is the way,
that leadeth to destruction,
and many there be which go in thereat:
Because strait is the gate, and narrow is
the way, which leadeth unto life,
and few there be that find it."

Narrow is the right way
And few are those therein
Not a lot of room here
No room for unrepented sin

For wide is the gate
And broad is the way
That leads to destruction
On that final day

Apples of Gold

September 8

Matthew 7:22-23

Many will say to me in that day, Lord, Lord, have we not prophesied in thy name? And in thy name have cast out devils? And in thy name done many wonderful works? And then will I profess unto them I never knew you: depart from me, ye that work iniquity."

There will be many people
Who will be in great surprise
On the day they see Jesus
And look into his eyes

He'll say I never knew you
Though you thought you served me well
And now because of your evil heart
You are being turned over to hell

Apples of Gold

September 9

Matthew 10:34

"Think not that I am come to send peace on earth: I came not to send peace, but a sword."

Jesus said in his own words
He came to bring a sword
To separate us from the world
Which will surely cause discord

But there comes a time in every life
When we must decide
Do we want to be a friend to the world
Or with Jesus ever abide

Apples of Gold

September 10

Matthew 10:36

"And a man's foes shall be they of his own household."

Sometimes for our enemies
We need not look at a distance
They are in our own homes
In our daily existence

So always be open
To what the Lord is showing you
Else the enemy can adversely effect
All you say and do

Apples of Gold

September 11

Matthew 11:28

"Come unto me, all ye that labour and are heavy laden, and I will give you rest."

When life gets heavy
And the labor gets hard
Come home to Jesus
Come home to the Lord

His burden is easy
His yoke is light
And he will give you back
Your spiritual sight

Apples of Gold

September 12

Matthew 24:24

"For there shall arise false Christs, and false prophets and shall shew great signs and wonders; insomuch that , if it were possible, they shall deceive the very elect."

We need to be grounded
We need to be close
For all the false prophets
Want to deceive us most

For Satan knows
He has but little time
To cause us to stumble
And make us fall behind

Apples of Gold

September 13

Exodus 20:20

"Fear not; for God is come to prove you, and that his fear may be before your faces, that ye sin not."

When the Lord comes to prove you
It's always out of love
For your heavenly Father
Wants you to be with him,
in his home above

He comes to us to purge
And to prove and test
So that in the end
We might be firmly blessed

Apples of Gold

September 14

Exodus 23:20

"Behold, I send an Angel before thee, to keep thee in the way, and to bring thee into the place which I have prepared."

He's prepared a place for us above
A place on earth below
And if we will but seek his face
We'll experience both of them I know

And he will keep you in the way
He's sent his Angel to lead
So that he could hold your hand
And meet your every need

Apples of Gold

September 15

Exodus 33:17

"...I will do this thing also that thou hast spoken; for thou hast found grace in my sight, and I know thee by name."

Oh, the precious love of Jesus
He knows us by our name
He never will forsake or leave us
He will always be the same

He says he will do the thing
Of which we have spoken
He came to confirm his word
And that it might not be broken

Apples of Gold

September 16

Exodus 34:10

"And he said, Behold , I make a covenant; before all thy people I will do marvels, such as have not been done in all the earth, nor in any nation: and all the people among which thou art shall see the work of the Lord: for it is a terrible thing that I will do with thee."

What the Lord is about to do
Is going to be a surprise
The multitudes will not believe
What they are seeing with their eyes

It's going to be a terrible thing
What he will do with thee
As a matter of fact there's a possibility
It will shock even you and me.

Apples of Gold

September 17

Numbers 16:28

"...Hereby ye shall know that the Lord hath sent me to do all these works; for I have not done them of mine own mind."

When you're doing what the Lord has said
Many shall point and doubt
But when his master plan is revealed
There will be ample reason to shout

He has a way of acknowledging
The ones that he has sent
And putting his seal of approval on you
Before your life is spent

Apples of Gold

September 18

Numbers 23:19

"God is not a man, that he should lie; neither the son of man, that he should repent: hath he said, and shall he not do it? Or hath he spoken, and shall he not make it good?"

If the Lord has given you a promise
It's as good as done
For none of his promises shall fail
No, not a single one

So trust the Lord with all your heart
Do your best to obey
Then stand back and watch what happens
And try not to get in his way

Apples of Gold

September 19

Numbers 32:23

"…be sure your sin shall find you out."

If you think you can sin in secret
And believe it can't be known
Your Fathers about to show you
He's setting on the throne

Nothing you do in darkness
Can from him be hidden
So take not unto yourself
Those things that are forbidden

Apples of Gold

September 20

Joshua 1:14

"...but ye shall pass before your brethren armed, all the mighty men of valour, and help them;"

If the Lord has equipped you
And taught you how to fight
You must now help your brethren
To gain their spiritual might

You have gone before them
So that you might know
How to navigate this journey
And the pitfalls to them show

Apples of Gold

September 21

Joshua 3:4

"...for ye have not passed this way heretofore."

When we're on a path
That we have not trod before
God will hold our hand
Of that you can be sure

He knows the way to go
So keep your eyes on Jesus
He promises in the word
He will never forsake or leave us

Apples of Gold

September 22

Joshua 17:18

"...for thou shalt drive out the Canannites, though they have iron chariots, and though they be strong."

Though your enemy has Iron Chariots
Though they be strong
Your Father will not allow them
To get away with any wrong

They may prosper for a season
They may prosper for a night
But when the battle's over
You'll find you won the fight

Apples of Gold

September 23

2 Samuel 8:14

"...And the Lord preserved David whithersoever he went."

The Lord knows how to keep us
No matter where we go
He's always watching over us
His love for us to show

So if you're forced to walk
In a new and untried way
Be sure that he is with you
Every single day

Apples of Gold

September 24

2 Samuel 14:14

"For we must needs die, and are as water spilt on the ground which cannot be gathered up again; neither doth God respect any person: yet doth he devise means, that his banished be not expelled from him."

Banished but not expelled
These words caught me when I was falling
I thought I had missed the mark
I thought I had missed my calling

I thought I was eternally lost
Fallen from his grace
This scripture let me know
One day I would surely see his face

Apples of Gold

September 25

2 Samuel 15:6

"And on this manner did Absalom to all Israel that came to the king for judgment; so Absalom stole the hearts of the men of Israel."

Absalom, Absalom
Stealing the hearts of men
Oh, what a hypocrite
Oh, what a sin

I to have met some Absaloms
Backstabbers shall we say
But they will reap their just rewards
On that great and glorious day

Apples of Gold

September 26

2 Samuel 16:12

"It may be that the Lord will look on mine affliction, and that the Lord will requite me good for this cursing this day."

God can take a cursing
And turn it for my good
No matter how hated I am
No matter how misunderstood

So let the enemy curse
And say what he may please
The worst it can do to me
Is drive me to my knees

Apples of Gold

September 27

2 Samuel 22:1-15

"The Lord thundered from heaven, and the most High uttered his voice. And he sent out arrows, and scattered them; lightning, and discomfited them."

The Lord moves through thunder
and lightning
All throughout the scripture
I think he's telling us something
I think he's painting a picture

So when you see the lightning flash
And hear the thunder roar
We'll know it's not just a storm
God is doing something more

Apples of Gold

September 28

2 Samuel 22:29

"For thou art my lamp O Lord; and the Lord will lighten my darkness."

When it's dark all around you
Before and behind
Don't fret or get worried
For the sun is about to shine

The Lord is our lamp
The Lord is our light
The Lord will go with us
Through every fear and every fight

Apples of Gold

September 29

2 Samuel 22:47

"The Lord liveth; and blessed be my rock; and exalted be the God of the rock of my salvation."

The God of my salvation
What a beautiful thought
His works he has shown me
His ways he has taught

He is our living rock
In whom we can trust
And in order to please him
Trust him we must

Apples of Gold

September 30th

1 Kings 11:6

"And Solomon did evil in the sight of the Lord, and went not fully after the Lord, as did David his father."

Are we following him fully
Or just half hearted
Are we clinging to him closely
Or have we from him departed

Solomon did not obey
All the Lord's decrees
And in the end it cost him
This should drive us to our knees

Apples of Gold

October 1

1 Corinthians 1:27

"But God hath chosen the foolish things of the world to confound the wise; and God hath chosen the weak things of the world to confound the things which are mighty;"

God uses the foolish things
The things that are weak
To confound the mighty
So his face, they will seek

It's not our wisdom
It's not our fame
It is his Spirit
That glorifies his name

Apples of Gold

October 2

1 Corinthians 3:19

"For the wisdom of this world is foolishness with God. For it is written, He taketh the wise in their own craftiness."

You may think you're wise in this world
And think yourself quite clever
But that will do you no good in
the spirit realm
Not now, No, not ever

So seek the Lord's wisdom
And not your own
For it is God
And God alone, who sits on the throne

Apples of Gold

October 3

1 Corinthians 6:9-10

"Know ye not that the unrighteous shall not inherit the kingdom of God? Be not deceived; neither fornicators, nor idolaters, nor adulterers, nor effeminate, nor abusers of themselves with mankind, Nor thieves, nor covetous, nor drunkards, nor revilers, nor extortioners, shall inherit the kingdom of God.

Make no mistake
There will be no sin in heaven
For all it takes to corrupt the whole
Is just a little leaven

So if your sin is listed
Or if your sin is not
Ask the Lord for forgiveness
For hell is awful hot

Apples of Gold

October 4

1 Corinthians 6:20

"For ye are bought with a price; therefore glorify God in your body, and in your spirit, which are God's."

If you have been purchased
By Jesus precious blood
You will escape destruction
Like Noah in the flood

But if you do not know him
You can meet him today
Ask him to be your Savior
And he will show you the way

Apples of Gold

October 5

1 Corinthians 11:3

"But I would have you know, that the head of every man is Christ; and the head of the woman is the man; and the head of Christ is God."

God's perfect order
Has always worked just fine
So we should take his order
And make it yours and mine

For if we're out of order
Nothing will work right
There will be strife and contention
And every day will be a fight

Apples of Gold

October 6

1 Corinthians 11:32

"But when we are judged, we are chastened of the Lord, that we should not be condemned with the world."

The Lord will chasten
Those that are his own
Deliver us from the world
And gather us round his throne

For if we are not chastened
To him we don't belong
Those who teach the opposite
Have surely gotten it wrong

Apples of Gold

October 7

1 Corinthians 15:58

"Therefore, my beloved brethren,
be ye stedfast, unmoveable, always
abounding in the work of the Lord,
forasmuch as ye know that your labour
is not in vain in the Lord."

If we labor for the Lord
Our labor is never in vain
For as sure as we suffer dark clouds
We shall also have the blessing of rain

For if we work for Jesus
We'll reap what we have sown
And the reward for our service
In our lives, will be known

Apples of Gold

October 8

Galatians 3:3

"Are ye so foolish? Having begun in the Spirit, are ye now made perfect by the flesh?

We began in the Spirit
With forgiveness full and free
And then try to work
For what he's already given you and me

So let us remember
He loved us while we were sinners
And in light of eternity
He knows we're just beginners

Apples of Gold

October 9

Galatians 6:9

"And let us not be weary in well doing:
for in due season we shall reap,
if we faint not."

Let us not grow weary
While working for the Lord
For we know that if we faint not
We shall reap a great reward

He says in his word
He'll give us strength for our day
So let us take courage
And continue on our way

Apples of Gold

October 10

Ephesians 4:26-27

**"Be angry, and sin not;
let not the sun go down upon your wrath;
Neither give place to the devil."**

*The devil is always looking
For a way into your life
And one sure way he can get in
Is through contention and strife*

*So deal with wrath and anger
Before the sun goes down
So that by the morning light
The enemy can't be found*

Apples of Gold

October 11

Ephesians 5:15-16

"See then that ye walk circumspectly, not as fools, but as wise, Redeeming the time, because the days are evil."

We need to redeem the time
For these are wicked days
Therefore we must teach others
Of our God and of his ways

Days on earth are growing shorter
The rapture drawing near
Let us be about the Father's business
For our mission on earth is clear

Apples of Gold

October 12

Ephesians 6:12

"For we wrestle not against flesh and blood, but against principalities, against powers, against the rulers of the darkness of this world, against spiritual wickedness in high places."

If you're a born again Christian
Your enemy is spiritual indeed
And learning to be a spiritual warrior
Is truly what you need

We have all been drafted
Whether we know it or not
Into this spiritual warfare
For that is our lot

Apples of Gold

October 13

Philippians 1:6

"Being confident of this very thing, that he which hath begun a good work in you will perform it until the day of Jesus Christ;"

Be sure of one thing
He will never quit on you
If you are born again
He will surely see you through

He will perform his promise
Until the very last day
For in his word he says
I am the truth, the life, and the way

Apples of Gold

October 14

Philippians 2:3

"Let nothing be done through strife or vainglory; but in lowliness of mind let each esteem other better than themselves."

In everything we do
Let us glorify the Lord
Like the children in the upper room
Let us be in one accord

Seek for ourselves
Not fortune and fame
May we only seek
To glorify his name

Apples of Gold

October 15

Philippians 4:8

"Finally, brethren, whatsoever things are true, whatsoever things are honest, whatsoever things are just, whatsoever things are pure, whatsoever things are lovely, whatsoever things are of good report; if there be any virtue, and if there be any praise, think on these things."

He tells us what to think about
That will give us peace of mind
What a loving God he must be
To be so concerned and kind

He knows that if we think about
These things so holy and pure
It will give us a quite spirit
And make our calling and election sure

Apples of Gold

October 16

Colossians 3:2

"Set your affection on things above, not on things on the earth."

Set your affection on things above
Not on things of earth
For the things of heaven, the things above
Are the only things with eternal worth

The things on earth below
Can easily rot and rust
But on the things in heaven above
We can truly place our trust

Apples of Gold

October 17

1 Thessalonians 5:22

"Abstain from all appearance of evil."

Let us pay attention
To what we watch and view
And see how often the appearance of evil
Is touching me and you

So in light of this scripture
Hmmm, let me see
Should we be watching everything
We are watching on TV?

Apples of Gold

October 18

2 Thessalonians 3:3

"But the Lord is faithful, who shall stablish you, and keep you from evil."

The Lord he is faithful
He will establish you
Watch over you all day
Help in everything you do

He will warn you of evil
Whisper in your ear
Tell you of certain things
You are getting too near

Apples of Gold

October 19

1Timothy 6:7-8

"For we brought nothing into this world, and it is certain we can carry nothing out. And having food and raiment let us be therewith content."

We can take nothing with us
When to the grave we go
Our status in life won't matter
Whether high or low

The only thing that will matter
Is what we did with Jesus
Did we invite him into our heart
Or did we tell him to leave us

Apples of Gold

October 20

1Timothy 6:9-10

"But they that will be rich fall into temptation and a snare, and into many foolish and hurtful lusts, which drown men in destruction and perdition. For the love of money is the root of all evil; which while some coveted after, they have erred from the faith, and pierced themselves through with many sorrows."

For the love of money
Some have gone astray
Pierced themselves through with sorrows
While going the wrong way

So let us seek wisdom
Like Solomon of old
For that is much wiser
Than seeking for silver and gold

Apples of Gold

October 21

1Timothy 6:20-21

"O Timothy, keep that which is committed to thy trust, avoiding profane and vain babblings, and oppositions of science falsely so called; Which some professing have erred concerning the faith..."

Let us not err through science
Vain babbling and such
For our precious faith
Is worth way to much

Let us never trade our faith
For the theories of man
For our faith was a gift
From God's own hand

Apples of Gold

October 22

Psalms 135:6

"Whatsoever the Lord pleased, that did he in heaven, and in earth, in the seas, and all deep places."

Whatever the Lord hath pleased
He has done today
Try to thwart his plan my brother
You will find no way

He sets on the throne
Ruling and reigning
And we cannot move his hand
With all our complaining

Apples of Gold

October 23

Psalms 138:8

"The Lord will perfect that which concerneth me; thy mercy, O Lord, endureth for ever; forsake not the works of thine own hands."

We all have imperfections
But we need not worry
For the Lord will correct them
And He's not in a hurry

He's seen the mess we've made
The tangled webs we've weaved
And he is here to fix them
If we will only believe

Apples of Gold

October 24

Psalms 138:7

"Though I walk in the midst of trouble, thou wilt revive me; thou shalt stretch forth thine hand against the wrath of mine enemies, and thy right hand shall save me."

When I'm surrounded by trouble
Enemies on all sides
The Lord will save me
If in him I abide

He'll raise one hand to stop my enemy
And one hand to save my life
And when he's finished there
He will drive out contention and strife

Apples of Gold

October 25

Psalms 139:4

"For there is not a word in my tongue, but, lo, O lord, thou knowest it altogether."

Before we say a word
You already know the sentence
Whether we are blessing another
Or pleading for our self repentance

Your ways are beyond knowing
As is your power
That is why we should seek your face
Every day and every hour

Apples of Gold

October 26

Psalms 141:3

"Set a watch, O Lord, before my mouth; keep the door of my lips."

We tend to say and speak
Things we shouldn't say
Therefore we need your help
To guard our lips everyday

So please Lord set a watch
Over these lips of mine
So that I speak not harsh words
Or to my brothers be unkind

Apples of Gold

October 27

Psalms 145:18-19

"The Lord is nigh unto all them that call upon him, to all that call upon him in truth. He will fulfil the desire of them that fear him; he also will hear their cry, and will save them."

If you are serious about God
He is serious about you
And the closer you draw to him
The closer he will draw too

He longs to fulfill your desires
And watch at your joyful surprise
He shows you things you know not of
To see that wonder fill your eyes

Apples of Gold

October 28

Proverbs 4:13

"Take fast hold of instruction; let her not go; keep her; for she is thy life."

When you receive instruction
Think not to let it go
For it may save your very life
And wisdom to you show

When God points you in a direction
Be sure it's for you best
If you know you have his word on it
Your spirit will be at rest

Apples of Gold

October 29

Proverbs 6:26

"For by means of a whorish woman
a man is brought to a piece of bread:
and the adultress will hunt for
the precious life."

Things may not always be
Exactly what they seem
Although they are pursuing you
Pulling down the anointing is their dream

They are just a pawn
In Satan's wicked hand
To pull down the man of God
And then disappear like sand

Apples of Gold

October 30

Proverbs 10:19

"In the multitude of words there wanteth not sin: but he that refraineth his lips is wise."

Some people think the more they talk
The wiser that they sound
But in a non stop flow of words
Sin can always be found

It surely may be possible
That the one who's slow to speak
Has gotten there through wisdom
By being humble and being meek

Apples of Gold

October 31

Proverbs 11:25

"…he that watereth shall be watered also himself."

When you minister to a brother
The blessing comes back on you
So be quick to water another
That you may be watered too

It's better to give than receive
This saying is true
So as we have preached
Let us therefore do

Apples of Gold

November 1

Proverbs 11:8

"The righteous is delivered out of trouble and the wicked cometh, in his stead."

The righteous are delivered
Of this we can be sure
For the Lord sees his motives
That they are true and pure

The wicked sometimes
Will come in their stead
And know not why they are falling
For the scriptures, they have not read

Apples of Gold

November 2

Proverbs 14:12

"There is a way which seemeth right unto a man, but the end thereof are the ways of death."

The way you are going
May look just right
So you are pursuing it
With all your might

But before you go too far
In the wrong direction
Be sure and pull our your map
For guidance and protection

Apples of Gold

November 3

Proverbs 15:16

"Better is little with the fear of the Lord than great treasure and trouble therewith."

We can't measure success
By earthly gain
For sometimes success
Brings heartache and pain

But the fear of the Lord
Brings joy and peace
Things money can't buy
To say the least

Apples of Gold

November 4

Proverbs 17:13

**"Whoso rewardeth evil for good,
evil shall not depart from his house."**

When someone does you good
Be sure you do the same
Otherwise evil
Will cling to your name

For the enemy can be in your house
As King David learned
Because for a moment of pleasure
The law of God he spurned

Apples of Gold

November 5

Genesis 3:1

"Now the serpent was more subtil than any beast of the field which the Lord God had made…"

Satan he works undercover
Always blaming another
A snake in the grass it seems
Shooting darts at the redeemed

It could come in the night,
it could in the day
God only knows it could come any way
Commit to no man Jesus said
And pray everyday for your daily bread

Apples of Gold

November 6

James 3:16

"For where envying and strife is, there is confusion and every evil work."

Where we see the jealousy
There will Satan be
Stirring up the saints of God
Causing strife for you and me

It's like an invitation
To Lucifer himself
To see his will accomplished
While putting God's will on the shelf

Apples of Gold

November 7

John 9:4

"I must work the works of him that sent me, while it is day; the night cometh, when no man can work."

I see the clouds a gathering
The sky is darkening fast
We must do the works of the Father
While our fading sunlight last

The night is drawing nearer
The day is almost done
The final harvest ready
The race is nearly run

Apples of Gold

November 8

Jeremiah 29:11

"For I know the thoughts that I think toward you, saith the Lord, thoughts of peace, and not of evil, to give you an expected end."

As many as the sands of the sea
So are my thoughts toward thee
You are the apple of my eye
I hear your every cry

Never hesitate to tell me
All your thoughts and care
For when you come before me
I am waiting for you there

Apples of Gold

November 9

1 Corinthians 1:18

"For the preaching of the cross is to them that perish foolishness; but unto us which are saved it is the power of God."

It may seem strange
To save the world through preaching
But God's ways are not our ways
Is what to you, I'm teaching

He gave unto us all
The freedom of choice
And those who will be saved
Will hearken to his voice

Apples of Gold

November 10

Joel 2:25

**"And I will restore to you the years
that the locust hath eaten,
the cankerworm, and the caterpillar,
and the palmerworm…"**

The years, they may seem wasted
Spent in vanity and pride
And in our bitter sorrow
We find no place to hide

But God is somehow able
Through his love and power
To restore to us through his plan
Every single hour

Apples of Gold

November 11

Numbers 13:30

"And Caleb stilled the people before Moses, and said, Let us go up at once, and possess it; for we are well able to overcome it."

When those around you stumble
And say we're sure to fail
Keep your eyes of Jesus
It will cause you to prevail

If you seem out numbered
And your effort seems so small
Remember God gives the victory
With him you cannot fall

Apples of Gold

November 12

John 19:11

"Jesus answered, Thou couldest have no power at all against me, except it were given thee from above..."

Our enemies cannot touch us
Lest the Lord, he gives them leave
Cannot snare or trap us
Through the tangled web they weave

Our Lord sets in the heavens
He's calling all the shots
He will have them in derision
And tie their plans in knots

Apples of Gold

November 13

Proverbs 16:18

"Pride goeth before destruction,
and an haughty spirit before a fall."

When we think to highly
Of the man we've come to be
The Father knows how to humble us
And make us see our need

Be careful how you think
Of what you say and do
Lest the Lord, must come to deal
With pride in me and you

Apples of Gold

November 14

Proverbs 16:25

"There is a way that seemeth right unto a man, but the end thereof are the ways of death."

There is a way that seems OK
When just the surface you see
But when you look beyond the front
The ending is not what it seemed to be

Therefore, we must seek the Lord Jesus
He's the way, the truth, the life
He will lead us to the Father
Away from all the sin and strife

Apples of Gold

November 15

Proverbs 18:10

"The name of the Lord is a strong tower: the righteous runneth into it, and is safe."

There is a place of safety
In the world it's little known
It's an ark made of promises
Its foundation is a stone

The stone, his name is Jesus
This stone cannot be shaken
Those who enter in
Will not be forsaken

Apples of Gold

November 16

Daniel 1:8

"But Daniel purposed in his heart that he would not defile himself with the portion of the king's meat, nor with the wine which he drank: therefore he requested of the prince of the eunuchs that he might not defile himself."

Long before his trial he knew
There were things he would not do
He decided to have a clear, clean mind
Was better than the worlds richest find

For if we gain the whole world
And lose our own soul
What have we accomplished
What was our goal

Apples of Gold

November 17

Proverbs 25:11

"A word fitly spoken is like apples of gold in pictures of silver."

People need nourishment
We're often told
But more than that
They need Apples of Gold

A word fitly spoken
Can set a soul free
From all of the lying
Done by our enemy

Thus the title
Of my little book
Which I pray brings you blessing
When in it you look

Apples of Gold

November 18

Exodus 23:2

"Thou shalt not follow a multitude to do evil…"

When all around us are gone astray
  And the lines, becoming gray
  There is still a God in heaven
  Who bids us, go his way

And when we follow his command
  Striving for the right
  He will lend a helping hand
  And we shall win the fight

Apples of Gold

November 19

Deuteronomy 11:26-28

"Behold, I set before you this day a blessing and a curse; A blessing, if ye obey the commandments of the Lord your God, which I command you this day: And a curse, if ye will not obey the commandments of the Lord your God...."

We all must make a choice
Whom we will serve
For which there are consequences
That we deserve

But God allows U turns
If we have gone the wrong way
Takes us back in his arms
And allows us there, to stay

Apples of Gold

November 20

1 Timothy 5:19

"Against an elder receive not an accusation, but before two or three witnesses."

Satan is the accuser
But servants, he has many
Who come against the saints of God
To find fault, yes any

But God in his mercy
Gave us this scripture
To let us know
Takes more than one to paint a picture

Apples of Gold

November 21

Hebrews 9:27

"And as it is appointed unto men once to die, but after this the judgment:"

One life is all we have
To find the path to the Father
Jesus he's the only way
Besides him there's no other

No time to cry, no time to plead
It's all been said and done
He will say to you enter in
Or, you did not accept my Son

No other question will there be
On the judgment day
He will say come in my child
To others, go away

Apples of Gold

November 22

Hebrews 12:28

"…let us have grace, whereby we may serve God acceptably with reverence and godly fear…"

Oh, for days gone by
Of reverence and godly fear
When all the nations trembled
As they knew that God drew near

But now that sinners are called seekers
And we don't preach hell so hot
Reverence and fear are fading
Whether we like it or not

Apples of Gold

November 23

1 John 4:1

"Beloved, believe not every spirit, but try the spirits whether they are of God; because many false prophets are gone out into the world."

If it makes you tingle
And gives you goose bumps, so rare
This does not mean it's from heaven
It could be from down there

Satan he can counterfeit
The miracles of the Lord
We must test and try our feelings
According to the word

Apples of Gold

November 24

1 Chronicles 17:23

"Therefore now, Lord, let the thing that thou hast spoken concerning thy servant and concerning his house be established for ever, and do as thou hast said."

When God gives us a promise
On it, we can rely
Do as thou has said, Oh Lord
Should be our only reply

He's not a man that he should lie
His promises are true
So if you've heard, thus saith the Lord
That he will surely do

Apples of Gold

November 25

Isaiah 34:8

"For it is the day of the Lord's vengeance, and the year of recompences for the controversy of Zion."

There's coming a day
I believe it is near
The books will all be opened
All faces filled with fear

Vengeance is mine thus saith the Lord
Today is the day of reckoning
Those of you who must depart
Hearkened not to my beckoning

Apples of Gold

November 26

Daniel 9:22

"And he informed me, and talked with me, and said, O Daniel, I am now come forth to give thee skill and understanding."

When we determine in our heart,
From Jesus, not to wander
He will give us understanding
And cause our heart to ponder

All the wonders of his love
The might of his creation
How a heart can be so tender
Yet rule the mighty nations

Apples of Gold

November 27

Micah 7:6

"…a man's enemies are the men of his own house."

This passage is a sad one
But, Oh how true
The enemy sometimes uses
Those closest to me and you

The children of disobedience
Are the ones he taps for service
Sometimes he must get ever so close
When he intends to usurp us

Apples of Gold

November 28

Matthew 24:4

"And Jesus answered and said unto them, Take heed that no man deceive you."

False prophets they are running to and fro
Disguised as minister of light
They secretly teach the wrong
While pretending to teach what's right

They have their own agenda
Their kingdom, they are trying to build
And to the word of God
They bid you not to yield

Apples of Gold

November 29

Mark 4:41

"…What manner of man is this, that even the wind and the sea obey him?"

There is a God in heaven
He is master of the sea
All nature must obey him
As he says, so shall it be

What manner of man
Is this in our boat
Who is able to keep,
All heaven and earth afloat

Apples of Gold

November 30

Luke 4:24

"And he said, Verily I say unto you, No prophet is accepted in his own country."

Some were too familiar
With the carpenter, Joseph's son
To realize he was their Savior
The one and only one

In his own country
He had very little respect
From this we should learn a lesson
Be careful whom you reject

Apples of Gold

December 1

Ester 3:5

"And when Haman saw that Mordecai bowed not, nor did him reverence, then was Haman full of wrath."

When to our enemy
We do not submit
We can, our life
To God commit

And when our enemy
Seeks to put us down
Hanging on his own gallows
He shall be found

Apples of Gold

December 2

Ruth 2:10

"...Why have I found grace in thine eyes, that thou shouldest take knowledge of me, seeing I am a stranger?"

Why did the Lord love me
When I was yet a stranger
Why did he save me
From all those hidden dangers

Was it because he loved me
While I was yet a sinner
And knew that one day
He would make me a winner

Apples of Gold

December 3

Psalms 105:5

"Remember his marvelous works that he hath done; his wonders, and the judgments of his mouth;"

When it seems the Lord is far away
From your troubles and your crying
Think of years gone by
When on the cross, he was dying

Remember his marvelous works
How he forgave your sin
Turn back to him and repent
And you will see his works again

Apples of Gold

December 4

Psalms 105:28

"He sent darkness, and made it dark and they rebelled not against his word."

When in darkness
You are sitting
His holy word,
Do not be forgetting

His word is stronger than the darkness
And light is on the way
Joy comes in the morning
There will be a brighter day

Apples of Gold

December 5

Psalms 1:1-2

"Blessed is the man that walketh not in the counsel of the ungodly, nor standeth in the way of sinners, nor sitteth in the seat of the scornful. But his delight is in the law of the Lord; and in his law doth he meditate day and night."

Satan comes with lies, a plenty
To try and trip you up
But if in the word, you have your delight
The Lord has filled your cup

With promises so sure, and words
so wonderful
That Satan has to flee
He cannot touch the blessed assurance
That Jesus gives you and me

Apples of Gold

December 6

Joshua 24:15

"And if it seem evil unto you to serve the Lord, choose you this day whom ye will serve"

Choose this day whom you will serve
You cannot serve two masters
If you try, believe me friend
It will surely bring disaster

But if you turn to the living God
He will gladly be your Father
Once you've served God almighty
You will never want another

Apples of Gold

December 7

John 1:29

"The next day John seeth Jesus coming unto him and saith, Behold the Lamb of God, which taketh away the sin of the world."

Behold the Lamb of God
Who came in total perfection
He gave his life for you and me
Without any objection

There is no other sacrifice
That could purchase your pardon
So please, be not like Pharaoh
And let you heart not be hardened

Apples of Gold

December 8

Psalms 3:3

"But thou, O Lord, art a shield for me; my glory, and the lifter up of mine head."

When my head is hanging down
There's one that lifts me up
Jesus is his precious name
He ever fills my cup

He is my shield and glory
My protection and my light
He's my eternal salvation
He makes my dimness bright

Apples of Gold

December 9

Jeremiah 29:13

**"And ye shall seek me, and find me,
when ye shall search for me
with all your heart."**

Seek the Lord with all your heart
And him you're sure to find
He will then wipe all your tears away
And bid you come and dine

He wants you at his table
Learning at his feet
He wants to heal your hurts
And make your life complete

Apples of Gold

December 10

Nahum 1:3

"The Lord is slow to anger, and great in power, and will not at all acquit the wicked; the Lord hath his way in the whirlwind and in the storm, and the clouds are the dust of his feet."

The Lord is slow to anger
He knows we are but dust
Ever ready to forgive us
Cleanse us as he must

He works in his great power
To draw us to his throne
He gave the life of his Son
To make us all his own

Apples of Gold

December 11

Psalms 3:6

"I will not be afraid of ten thousands of people, that have set themselves against me round about."

When a host rises up against me
Though they be a thousand strong
I will not fear, no never
For they will not last for long

My Father who holds all battles
In the palm of his hand
Has made it quite clear
Against me, the wicked can't stand

Apples of Gold

December 12

Psalms 4:8

"I will both lay me down in peace, and sleep: for thou Lord, only makest me dwell in safety."

My sleep shall be sweet
My safety shall be sure
For the Lord is my keeper
And through him I'll endure

I have peace like a river
It flows through my soul
Knowing he's ever watching me
And helping me reach my goal

Apples of Gold

December 13

Matthew 6:33

"But seek ye first the kingdom of God, and his righteousness; and all these things shall be added unto you."

Some seek money
Some seek fame
Wisdom bids us
To seek his name

For in our God
Our fullness dwells
And to our God
Our worship swells

Apples of Gold

December 14

Acts 9:15

"But the Lord said unto him, Go thy way; for he is a chosen vessel unto me, to bear my name before the Gentiles, and kings, and the children of Israel"

God chooses whom he will
It matters not their past
Whatever the list of sins
It's the blood that speaks at last

Though we are red like crimson
We shall be white as snow
It's not what we've done that matters
It's all in who we know

Apples of Gold

December 15

Psalms 76:10

"Surely the wrath of man shall praise thee; the remainder of wrath shalt thou restrain."

We tend to be disturbed
When the wrath of man we see
But as this scripture says
It should not bother you and me

Our Father uses wrath
To praise his prefect name
Any wrath left over
He simply shall restrain

Apples of Gold

December 16

John 3:30

"He must increase, but I must decrease."

He must be made larger
And I must become small
I must come to realize
He knows and made it all

So when at life
I start to fret
He says, peace is found in me
Please don't forget

Apples of Gold

December 17

John 4:6

"Now Jacob's well was there. Jesus therefore, being wearied with his journey, sat thus on the well: and it was about the sixth hour."

Jesus himself, the Son of God
Even at times felt weary
None of us are exempt
From days that grow long and dreary

His strength will come
When our strength is gone
And like Paul we can say
When I am weak, then I am strong

Apples of Gold

December 18

Acts 4:25

"...Why did the heathen rage, and the people imagine vain things?"

Our enemies make master plans
To bring us down in defeat
But their plans turn to vanity
When our protector they meet

The heathen twist and shout
And make a lot of noise
But they accomplish no more than children
Playing with their toys

Apples of Gold

December 19

Acts 10:4

"…Thy prayers and thine alms are come up for a memorial before God."

Thy prayers go not unnoticed
Thy giving is noted as well
The Father, he is watching
As the ship gets ready to sail

The old ship of Zion is boarding
I believe she is almost ready
Soon we will be departing
On a course that is straight and steady

Apples of Gold

December 20

Hosea 4:6

"My people are destroyed for lack of knowledge"

Seek the Lord with all your heart
From his knowledge do not depart
He will lead and guide us
When his face we seek

He's the master teacher
His knowledge he will impart
To keep the enemy from destroying us
To keep us from losing heart

Apples of Gold

December 21

Mark 4:40

"...Why are ye so fearful? How is it that ye have no faith?"

If you belong to Jesus
You have nothing to fear
For when your trials overwhelm you
Jesus is ever so near

Run to him with your questions
He will be right there
To solve all your problems
And put at rest all your care

Apples of Gold

December 22

Hosea 5:15

"I will go and return to my place, till they acknowledge their offence, and seek my face: in their affliction they will seek me early."

The Lord is waiting
In his place
Until we acknowledge our sin
To his face

When we admit to him
What we have done
He will come and sup with us
He and his Son

Apples of Gold

December 23

Mark 5:19

"...Go home to thy friends, and tell them how great things the Lord hath done for thee, and hath had compassion on thee."

What has the Lord done for you
Whom have you told
Keeping silent your testimony
Is like hording pure gold

Another man may need it
More than you think
Like a dying man in the desert
Who is desperate without a drink

Apples of Gold

December 24

Luke 1:52

"He hath put down the mighty from their seats, and exalted them of low degree."

God will always right the wrong
About that there's no doubt
He will lift the lowly up
He will cast the mighty out

We will either see it here below
Or in heaven up above
But either way, there's no denying
The Father's perfect love

Apples of Gold

December 25

Acts 4:12

"Neither is there salvation in any other; for there is none other name under heaven given among men, whereby we must be saved."

They say we must be tolerant
And believe there's many ways
To get to God in heaven
When we've finished all our days

But the living word, it tells me
This cannot be true
For salvation for my soul, Jesus
Is only found in you

Apples of Gold

December 26

Mark 10:29-30

"And Jesus answered and said, Verily I say unto you, there is no man that hath left house, or brethren, or sisters, or father, or mother, or wife, or children, or lands, for my sake, and the gospel's, But he shall receive an hundredfold now in this time, houses, and brethren, and sisters, and mothers, and children, and lands, with persecutions; and in the world to come eternal life."

If you have lost a single thing
For the gospels sake
You shall receive a hundred fold
On this you can surely bank

The Lord will owe us nothing
When alls been said and done
We will owe him eternal thanks
For the gift of his precious Son

Apples of Gold

December 27

Romans 5:8

"But God commendeth his love toward us, in that, while we were yet sinners, Christ died for us."

While I was yet a sinner
Not knowing right from wrong
The Lord loved me dearly
And suffered with me long

All the time knowing
One day I would return
To the God of my fathers
And say, the lesson has been learned

Apples of Gold

December 28

1 Corinthians 1:18

"For the preaching of the cross is to them that perish foolishness; but unto us which are saved it is the power of God."

Preaching saves some
Others it condemns
Because some shun the message
Others just run to him

Only two kinds of people
The saved and the lost
But for every one of them
Jesus paid the cost

Apples of Gold

December 29

1 Corinthians 11:3

**"But I would have you know,
that the head of every man is Christ;
and the head of the woman is the man;
and the head of Christ is God."**

God put all things in order
That order still stands today
No matter what modern man may say
This is still God's way

His way is the right way
To this we must confess
And once we've tried his methods
We will know they work the best

Apples of Gold

December 30

2 Corinthians 11:14-15

"And no marvel; for Satan himself is transformed into an angel of light. Therefore it is no great thing if his ministers also be transformed as the ministers of righteousness; whose end shall be according to their works."

Be not to surprised
If in the pulpit you see
A minister being transformed
Into darkness before thee

Paul said it could happen
In this little verse
Satan working behind the scenes
It's all part of the curse

Apples of Gold

December 31

Romans 5:19

"For as by one man's disobedience many were made sinners, so by the obedience of one shall many be make righteous."

Because of Adam's sin
The state of man did fall
But through his grace and mercy
Jesus did answer the call

The call to be the offering
Through his righteous sinless blood
And make the way available
To escape the evil flood

Index of Scripture Texts

Chapter/Verse Date

Genesis
32:34	*1/20*
41:51	*12/21*
41:52	*2/22*
26:22	*6/11*
31:16	*6/12*
3:1	*11/5*

Exodus
18:11	*1/15*
1:21	*2/15*
3:7	*2/24*
20:20	*7/9, 9/13*
23:20	*7/10, 9/14*
23:2	*7/11, 11/18*
23:30	*7/12*
22:29	*7/13*
33:17	*7/14, 9/15*
34:10	*9/16*

Leviticus
18:22	*6/9*

Chapter/Verse Date

Numbers
13:30	*2/25, 11/11*
12:2	*6/25*
16:28	*9/17*
23:19	*9/18*
32:33	*9/19*

Deuteronomy
4:37	*2/20*
8:3	*5/21*
15:7	*8/13*
11:26	*11/19*

Joshua
1:14	*9/20*
3:4	*9/21*
17:18	*9/22*
24:15	*12/6*

Ruth
4:15	*7/17*
2:10	*7/16, 12/2*

Apples of Gold

Chapter/Verse Date

1 Samuel
15:23	6/18
24:12	6/19
10:7	7/30
11:9	7/31
12:16	8/1
12:21	8/2
12:24	8/3
14:6	8/4
15:22	8/5

2 Samuel
15:11	3/18
8:14	9/23
14:14	9/24
15:6	9/25
16:12	9/26
22:14-15	9/27
22:29	9/28
22:47	9/29

1 Kings
11:6	9/30

2 Kings
8:6	2/5
1:3	4/9, 7/1
12:5	4/10
17:9	4/11
17:33	4/12
17:39	4/13
19:22	4/14
2:21	6/13

Chapter/Verse Date

1 Chronicles
17:2	1/13
16:11	6/20
17:23	6/26, 11/24

2 Chronicles
20:6	1/22

Ester
3:51	2/1

Psalms
50:16	1/14
139:17-1	2/6
41:1-2	2/19
5:12	3/12
105:28	4/30, 12/4
3:6	6/8
30:11	6/21
55:21	6/22
119:67	6/23
119:165	6/24
126:6	7/15
7:15-16	8/14
144:1	8/15
135:6	10/22
138:8	10/23
138:7	10/24
139:4	10/25
141:3	10/26
145:18-19	10/27
1:1-2	12/3
53:3	12/4
3:6	12/11
4:8	12/12
76:10	12/15

Apples of Gold

Chapter/Verse	*Date*	*Chapter/Verse*	*Date*

Proverbs
14:12	*3/13, 11/2*
15:27	*5/1*
4:3	*10/28*
6:26	*10/29*
10:19	*10/30*
11:25	*10/31*
11:8	*11/1*
15:16	*11/3*
17:13	*11/4*
16:18	*11/14*
18:10	*11/15*
25:11	*11/17*

Ecclesiastes
5:5-6	*5/22*

Isaiah
19:20	*3/14*
42:19-20	*5/23*
48:17	*7/18*
54:17	*7/19*
343:8	*11/25*

Jeremiah
5:25	*1/3*
10:2	*1/23*
10:12	*3/15*
51:36	*3/16*
32:27	*3/19*
1:8	*5/7*
1:17	*5/8*
32:19	*7/20*
29:13	*12/9*

Lamentations
3:25	*1/21*

Ezekiel
21:16	*1/16*
17:24	*5/14*
16:49	*5/24*
3:17	*6/10*
33:33	*7/2*
13:3	*6/14*
3:8-9	*8/16*

Daniel
11:32	*1/24*
2:28	*3/17*
2:21	*3/20*
5:20	*7/21*
1:8	*11/16*
9:22	*11/26*

Hosea
4:6	*12/20*
5:15	*12/22*

Joel
2:25	*11/10*

Amos
5:4	*5/16*
8:11	*5/17*

Jonah
2:7	*3/21, 5/19*
1:9	*5/18*

Chapter/Verse	Date	Chapter/Verse	Date
Micah		**Matthew (cont.**	
7:6	11/27	5:16	3/8
		6:16	3/9
Nahum		6:24	3/10, 9/6
1:3	8/17, 12/10	6:31	3/11
		10:36	3/30, 9/10
Habakkuk		11:28	3/31, 9/11
3:17-18	3/22	13:49	4/1
2:1	7/22	3:17 & 4:1	7/3
		8:13	7/4
Zephaniah		5:17	9/5
2:3	3/26, 8/28	7:13-14	9/7
1:12	8/27	7:22-23	9/8
1:14	8/29	10:34	9/9
		24:24	9/12
Haggai		24:4	11/29
2:4	3/23, 8/6	6:33	12/13
2:19	8/7		
		Mark	
Zechariah		1:7	1/8
4:6	3/24	2:17	1/29, 4/2
4:10	3/25, 9/1	4:9	4/3
2:8	3/27, 8/30	4:41	4/4, 11/29
4:7	8/31	6:3	4/5
11:17	9/2	7:6	4/6
		7:37	4/7
Malachi		9:23	4/8, 7/25
3:6-7	3/28	1:17	5/25
3:7	9/3	4:40	6/15, 12/21
3:8	9/4	8:23	7/23
		7:33	7/24
Matthew		5:19	12/23
4:4	3/5, 3/29	10:29-30	12/26
4:16	3/6		
4:17	3/7		

Chapter/Verse Date

Luke
1:45	1/25
22:31-32	2/12
18:1	5/9
3:10	5/26
9:1	6/16
9:62	8/8
4:24	11/30
1:52	12/24

John
7:7	1/26, 5/28, 8/20
20:25	2/7
13:7	5/2
15:15	5/20
13:34-35	5/29
6:17	7/5
9:4	7/6
7:43	7/26
3:27	8/18
6:17	8/21
6:24	8/22
8:7	8/23
8:11	8/24
8:32	8/25
9:35	8/26
9:4	11/7
19:11	11.12
1:29	12/7
3:30	12/16
4:6	12/17

Acts
13:2	1/17, 1/30
22:15	2/9

Chapter/Verse Date

Acts (cont.
12:43	5/3
5:41	5/4
12:11	5/27
10:4	7/7, 12/19
10:31	7/8
18:9-10	7/27
10:34	8/9
13:2	8/19
9:15	12/14
4:25	12/18
4:12	12/24

Romans
3:23	1/27, 5/30
8:31	2/13, 5/31
4:20-21	5/5
5:8	5/6, 12/27
16:17	5/10, 8/10
10:9	6/1
10:13	6/2
12:1	6/3
5:19	12/31

1 Corinthians
6:20	1/1, 4/16, 10/4
15:58	2/8, 4/19, 6/28, 10/7
4:10	4/15
7:23	4/17
11:3	4/18, 10/5, 12/29
16:9	4/20, 6/27
2:14	8/12
1:18	8/11
1:27	10/1
3:19	10/2

Chapter/Verse — Date

1 Corinthians (cont.
6:9-10	10/3
11:32	10/6
1:18	11/9, 12/28

2 Corinthians
3:5-6	4/21
4:8-9	4/22
4:13	4/23
5:17	4/24
10:3	4/25
10:4	4/26
11:14-15	4/27, 12/20
12:9	7/28

Galatians
6:7-8	½
6:2	1/9
1:9	1/28, 4/28, 6/4, 7/29
3:13	4/29
4:29	6/17
3:3	10/8
6:9	10/9

Ephesians
2:10	2/10
4:7	2/11
4:26-27	2/14, 10/10
5:15-16	10/11
6:12	10/12

Philippians
1:6	10/13
2:3	10/14
4:8	10/15

Chapter/Verse — Date

Colossians
2:8	2/15, 5/11
3:2	10/16

1 Thessalonians
5:22	10/17

2 Thessalonians
1:6	6/5
3:3	10/18

1 Timothy
2:12	1/10
4:1	5/12
6:10	5/13
6:7-8	10/19
6:9-10	10/20
6:20-21	10/21
5:19	11/20

2 Timothy
3:13	6/29

Titus
1:16	2/16

Philemon
Vs. 15	1/11

Hebrews
5:8	1/3
4:15-16	1/18
12:28	1/31, 11/22
11:5	2/17
9:27	11/21

Chapter/Verse Date

James
1:23-24   *1/12*
4:17   *6/30*
3:16   *11/6*

1 Peter
4:8   *1/19*
5:5   *3/4*
4:17   *6/6*

2 Peter
2:19   *3/2*
2:9   *3/3*

1 John
3:17   *1/4, 2/2*
4:4   *2/1*
4:1   *2/3*
4:18   *2/4*
4:12   *2/28*
2:16   *3/1*

3 John
Vs. 11   *2/27*

Jude
Vs. 3   *2/18*

Revelation
13:16-17   *1/5*
20:15   *1/6*
2:2 & 4   *2/26*
2:11   *6/7*

www.asheepspeaks.org